Commercial Property

Amending a Commercial Lease

For Jackie, Spider, Tato and Rooster

Commercial Property

Amending a Commercial Lease

Karl Bamford

LLB (Hons), Partner at Knight & Sons,
Newcastle-under-Lyme, Staffordshire

Butterworths
London, Edinburgh, Dublin
1998

United Kingdom	Butterworths, a Division of Reed Elsevier (UK) Ltd, Halsbury House, 35 Chancery Lane, LONDON WC2A 1EL and 4 Hill Street, EDINBURGH EH2 3JZ
Australia	Butterworths, a Division of Reed International Books Australia Pty Ltd, CHATSWOOD, New South Wales
Canada	Butterworths Canada Ltd, MARKHAM, Ontario
Hong Kong	Butterworths Asia (Hong Kong), HONG KONG
India	Butterworths Asia, NEW DELHI
Ireland	Butterworth (Ireland) Ltd, DUBLIN
Malaysia	Malayan Law Journal Sdn Bhd, KUALA LUMPUR
New Zealand	Butterworths of New Zealand Ltd, WELLINGTON
Singapore	Butterworths Asia, SINGAPORE
South Africa	Butterworths Publishers (Pty) Ltd, DURBAN
USA	Lexis Law Publishing, CHARLOTTESVILLE, Virginia

A CIP Catalogue record for this book is available from the British Library.

ISBN 0 406 90419 7

Printed by Hobbs the Printers Ltd, Totton, Hampshire

Preface

Within twelve months of qualifying as a solicitor and leaving London I accepted a job in a small corporate firm in Manchester. With the exception of one of the partners who dabbled in property work, I was on my own in this particular area of the law. I was ignorant and isolated. Like so many people do in such circumstances, I found solace in books, particularly those in the library dealing with property, and especially landlord and tenant where it appeared that a lot of my work was focused.

Some years later at Knight & Sons, one of the then trainees, and now one of my colleagues, Andrea Bruce, asked if I knew of any publication which would give her a quick insight into what amendments she should be making to a draft commercial lease which another of my colleagues had asked her to look at. Whilst I was able to point her in the direction of the priceless Landlord and Tenant (Business Tenancies) volumes of the *Encyclopaedia of Forms and Precedents* and also Murray Ross's excellent publication, *Drafting and Negotiating Commercial Leases* (Fourth Edition) (now in its Fifth Edition as *Ross: Commercial Leases)*, I had to admit I was not aware of anything which would act as a quick reference guide and sat down to help her. It was that conversation, as much as my initial isolation in Manchester, which made me think about how useful such a publication might be to a busy practitioner.

I considered the idea for such a publication for some time and eventually I contacted Butterworths with the idea for the book. The response I received from Liz Heathfield was so enthusiastic that any misgivings I had ever had quickly disappeared. Her enthusiasm acted as a catalyst, transforming my vague foggy ideas into something much more concrete. I owe her a very large debt of gratitude for having the confidence in both the idea and myself.

I am also deeply indebted to my senior partner, Tony Bell, for his support of the initial concept. He has also been a great source of encouragement throughout and his editorial input into the various drafts has been as important as his wise counsel and friendship. I did suggest that he should be a co-author, such has been his help, but in his usual minimalist way he laughed it off. Thanks Boss!

The book is not intended to be a detailed analysis of landlord and tenant law but a quick reference guide and aide memoire. I have generally kept case citations and discussions about the law to a minimum for this reason. While every lease needs to be looked at on its own merits and in all its surrounding circumstances, I hope the book will be useful to busy practitioners. I would recommend that legal advisers involve other professionals, especially surveyors, when they are trying to settle a lease. A failure to take account of the physical state of a building can have potentially disastrous financial implications for a tenant.

I would readily welcome comments and criticism from fellow practitioners, surveyors and anyone else who ever has recourse to the book.

While I have already acknowledged the roles of Liz Heathfield and Tony Bell there are one or two others I would like to thank. Firstly, Michelle '*Harry*' Walker whose word processing skills and support have been valuable and, secondly, Graham Williams of Taylor Joynson Garrett, one of my former colleagues in London. He probably doesn't know it yet, but he was the first to fire my enthusiasm for property law and proved to me that, while cynics might suggest otherwise, property work can actually be quite exciting and entertaining.

My final words are left for my wife Jackie and my three boys Sam, Tom and Jack for their patient forbearance whilst, '...Daddy is working on his book... again!'

Karl Bamford

Alsager
Stoke on Trent

December 1998

Contents

Table of statutory materials

Table of cases

DATE [   ] 19[   ]

1. [   ]

2. [   ]

3. [   ]

LEASE

relating to

[   ]

INDEX

DATE 199[ ]

PARTIES

1	**'Landlord'**	[ ] of [ ] whose registered office is at [ ] (Registered in England: Company Registration Number: [ ])
2	**'Original Tenant'**	[ ] of [ ] whose registered office is at [ ] (Registered in England: Company Registration Number: [ ])
3	**'Guarantor'**	[ ] of [ ] [whose registered office is at [ ]

OPERATIVE PROVISIONS

1 DEFINITIONS AND INTERPRETATION

For all purposes of this Lease (unless the context otherwise requires) the terms defined in this clause have the meanings specified

1.1	**'Accountant'**	[ ] or any other person who may be an employee of the Landlord or a Group Company but any person so appointed to act as an Accountant must be an Associate or Fellow of the Institute of Chartered Accountants in England and Wales
1.2	**'Additional Parking Bays'**	the parking bays numbered [ ] to [ ] inclusive in the car park of the Building shown [for the purposes of identification only] edged brown on Plan No 1
1.3	**'Adjoining Conduits'**	all the pipes, sewers, drains, mains, ducts, conduits, gutters, watercourses, wires, cables, channels, flues and all other conducting media and includes any fixings, louvres, cowls, covers and other ancillary apparatus that are in, on or under the Building and serve the Premises
1.4	**'Adjoining property of the Landlord'**	references to 'adjoining property of the Landlord' are references to each and every part of the neighbouring or adjoining land, excluding the Building, in which the Landlord or a Group Company has or during the Term acquires an interest or estate

COMMENTARY

PARTIES

If a company is a party to the lease (either as landlord, tenant or guarantor) it is essential that its company registration number and registered office are stated. It is important to be able to trace the relevant corporate party through what is often a maze of corporate transactions. The only certain way of doing this is to ensure company registration numbers (which are unique identity codes) are stated. The unique identification code of the company number is often used by some of the registries, eg HM Land Registry, and it also helps in making a search at Companies House. It is also essential to ensure that the company registered office is stated as this information is necessary to ensure compliance with the relevant provisions relating to service of notices, although a search at Companies House to check that it has not changed at the time of the search is obviously necessary. As a final point, if a corporate tenant is registered or stated as having an address offshore, it is good practice for an address for service in the UK to be given. A company search should reveal all relevant details.

OPERATIVE PROVISIONS

1.1 Any professional person called upon to perform any duty or function pursuant to the terms of the lease should be required to be a member of that profession's governing body, eg The Law Society, the Royal Institution of Chartered Surveyors etc. Not only will there be the requisite level of expertise but membership of such a body will ensure that any functions or duties undertaken pursuant to the terms of the lease are conducted within the ambit of the professional and ethical code laid down by that governing body. While there are various regulatory bodies for the accountancy profession, the Institute of Chartered Accountants in England and Wales is the author's preferred option.

1.2 Car parking spaces, particularly in relation to office accommodation, can be an emotive issue for tenants and their employees. It is absolutely vital that any parking bays or parking areas referred to in the lease as being for the use of the tenant, and the extent of any such rights, are accurately defined. As a tenant it is infinitely preferable to have the actual car parking spaces demised rather than simply being given a right to use them as the demise will confer exclusive possession of the parking bays on the tenant. As regards reference to the plan, or any plan, it is vital to state whether any verbal description of the premises, building, car parking space, etc is to take precedence over the plan or otherwise.

1.5	**'Building'**	all that the building known as [ ] and surrounding land shown for the purpose of identification only edged black on the Plan No 2
1.6	**'Common Parts'**	the areas and amenities made available from time to time by the Landlord for use in common by the tenants and occupiers of the Building and all persons expressly or by implication authorised by them including the pedestrian ways, forecourts, car parks, loading bays, service roads, landscaped areas, entrance halls, landings, lifts, lift-shafts, staircases, passages and areas designated for the keeping and collecting of refuse, but not limited to them PROVIDED ALWAYS that the landlord shall ensure at all times that sufficient areas of the common parts are available for use by the Tenant to enable the Tenant or any lawful sub-tenant to undertake its usual business at the Premises.
1.7	**'Conduits'**	the pipes, sewers, drains, mains, ducts, conduits, gutters, watercourses, wires, cables, laser optical fibres, data or impulse transmission, communication or reception systems, channels, flues and all other conducting media—including any fixings, louvres, cowls, covers and any other ancillary apparatus—that are in on over or under the Premises
1.8	**'Contractual Term'**	[ ] years from and including the day of 19 and ending at midnight on the day of 20
1.9	**'Decorating Years'**	[ ]
1.10	**'Development'**	References to 'development' are references to development as defined by the Town and Country Planning Act 1990 section 55
1.11	**'Group Company'**	a company that is a member of the same group as the Tenant within the meaning of the 1954 Act section 42
1.12	**'Guarantor'**	includes not only the person named above as the Guarantor, but also any person who enters into covenants with the Landlord pursuant to subclause 3.9.5.2 of clause 3.9.5 CONDITIONS or clause 3.22 REPLACEMENT GUARANTOR
1.13	**'Included Parking Bays'**	the parking bays numbered [ ] to [ ] inclusive in the car park of the Building, shown coloured green on the Plan No 1

1.5 The building as defined in the lease needs to be accurately identified by reference to a detailed plan.

1.6 It is vital that sufficient access is available to a tenant to secure use of the premises. The proviso added at the end of the clause achieves this.

1.8 Due to the legal rules relating to service of notices, whether pursuant to a rent review clause, option to determine or any other provision in the lease which requires a technical interpretation of dates, it is vital that the term commencement date is not open to doubt. The amendment proposed makes quite clear the date on which the term commences and the time and date when the term ends. If a term is stated to commence 'from' a certain date the general rule of law is that, in fact, it commences at the beginning of the following day and it ends at midnight on the anniversary of the date 'from' which it is granted. Although the courts have in several cases recently relaxed the very strict rules relating to compliance with strict timetables in favour of the 'reasonable recipient' test (see *Mannai Investment Co Ltd v Eagle Star Life Assurance Co Ltd* [1997] AC 749, HL and *Garston v Scottish Widows' Fund and Life Assurance Society* [1998] 3 All ER 596, CA) there is absolutely no need to leave anything in doubt and risk a claim for negligence.

1.11 While no amendment is suggested here it would have been had the definition of *Group Company* made reference to any statutory definition contained in either the Companies Act legislation or the taxation legislation which is much more restrictive as opposed to section 42 of the Landlord and Tenant Act 1954. The Landlord and Tenant Act 1954 gives much more flexibility.

1.14 **'Initial Provisional Service Charge'** £[ ] per year

1.15 **'Initial Rent'** the sum of £[ ] per year

1.16 **'Insurance Rent'** the Insurance Rent Percentage of the ~~gross~~ reasonable and proper sums net of any commission paid to, or discount received by, the Landlord ~~including any commission~~ that the Landlord is from time to time liable to pay:

(i) by way of premium for insuring the Building, including insuring for loss of rent, in accordance with his obligations contained in this Lease or, where the insurance includes the Building and other property, the proportion of those sums reasonably attributable to the Building

(ii) by way of premium for insuring in such amount and on such terms as the Landlord (acting reasonably) considers appropriate against all liability of the Landlord to third parties arising out of or in connection with any matter involving or relating to the Building and

(iii) for insurance valuations (but not more than once in any calendar year)

and all of any increased premium payable by reason of any act or omission of the Tenant or anyone at the Premises ~~with the Tenant's consent or any invitee employee or guest of the Tenant~~ and under the Tenant's control

1.15 Factual gaps in the draft lease must be carefully checked and completed by reference to the heads of terms agreed between the parties.

1.16 Insurance rent payments by the tenant should be by way of indemnity only. There should be no profit element or unjust enrichment for the landlord. If the gross premium purportedly payable by the landlord for insuring the premises is netted down to take account of any discounts allowed to him or commission paid to him then, clearly if the tenant makes the full gross repayment, there is a profit element for the landlord. The tenant should forcibly resist any attempt by the landlord to profit in this way. Indeed there may be circumstances where a tenant is able to get a better deal than the landlord, eg a retailer with a larger number of shops throughout the country. The tenant should strenuously resist any profiteering by the landlord although, as will be a recurring theme throughout the commentary, the relative bargaining strengths of the parties are in practice likely to be paramount. As the law currently stands there is no term to be implied, which means that any insurance premiums paid by the landlord must be reasonable (*Havenridge Ltd v Boston Dyers Ltd* [1994] 2 EGLR 73, CA) and it is vital therefore that the concept of reasonableness is introduced into the cost of such premiums.

1.16(i) The concept of reasonableness introduced here is self-explanatory and should not give the landlord cause for concern.

1.16(ii) Again, the concept of reasonableness here should not cause the landlord a problem. If the landlord is not prepared to accept an obligation to act reasonably then the tenant can, in the author's view, validly argue that the only implication to be drawn from this is that the landlord may seek to be unreasonable and perhaps a more serious question ought to be asked by the tenant about the basis of the relationship with the landlord on which he is about to embark. Is your client tenant willing to proceed with the lease on such a footing?

1.16(iii) Initially the tenant should resist an obligation to pay for valuations although the landlord's arguments are likely to win the day here. However, the tenant should not be obliged to pay for this more than once in any calendar year. If the landlord chooses to change his insurers (or brokers) that is a decision for the landlord, and the tenant should not be penalised in cost terms for this.

The amendment at the end of clause 1.16 (again to be a recurring theme throughout this commentary) seeks to mitigate the harsh effects of the wide class of persons covered by this clause as originally drafted. The landlord, perhaps understandably, wants the clause to be as wide as possible but the tenant's argument is that the tenant cannot be responsible, for example, for any member of the public, or contractor or licensee, who happens to wander into or be on the premises. There should be an element of control by the tenant and the amendment to this clause achieves this.

1.17	**'Insurance Rent Percentage'**	[ ] %
1.18	**'Insured Risks'**	the risks of loss or damage by fire, storm, tempest, earthquake, lightning, explosion, riot, civil commotion, malicious damage, impact by vehicles and by aircraft and articles dropped from aircraft (other than war risks), flood damage and bursting and overflowing of water pipes and tanks and such other risks whether or not in the nature of the foregoing against which a reasonably prudent landlord would normally insure~~, whether or not in the nature of the foregoing, as the Landlord from time to time decides to insure against~~
1.19	**'Interest'**	Unless the context requires otherwise, references to 'interest' are references to interest during the period from the date on which the payment is due to the date of payment, both before and after any judgment, at the Interest Rate then prevailing (where the interest rate is defined by reference to a bank base rate) or, should the base rate referred to in clause 1.20 'THE INTEREST RATE' cease to exist, at another reasonably comparable rate of interest ~~upon which the Landlord decides~~ closely comparable with the Interest Rate to be agreed between the parties or in default of agreement to be determined by the Accountant acting as an expert and not as an arbitrator
1.20	**'Interest Rate'**	the rate of 2% per year above the base lending rate of [ ] Bank plc or such other major clearing bank as the Landlord (acting reasonably) from time to time nominates in writing
1.21	**'Landlord'**	includes the person or persons from time to time entitled to possession of the Premises when this Lease comes to an end
1.22	**'Landlord's Expenses'**	the reasonable and proper costs and expenditure (including all charges, commissions, premiums, fees and interest) paid or incurred, or deemed in accordance with the provisions of Schedule 6 clause 2.3 DEEMED LANDLORD'S EXPENSES. to be paid or incurred, by the Landlord in respect of or incidental to all or any of the Services or otherwise required to be taken into account for the purpose of calculating the Service Charge

1.17. Although not a specifically suggested amendment, the tenant's adviser should be aware of the circumstances in which a stated percentage should be capable of being varied, eg if the landlord chose to extend or demolish part of the building of which the let premises form part. A suggested amendment would be: '*...as varied from time to time pursuant to part [ ] of Schedule [ ].*'

1.18 The risks for the tenant in relation to this clause as originally drawn are quite clear. If damage is caused to the property by anything other than an *insured risk* then, on the basis that the lease is a full repairing and insuring one, any such damage will fall to be repaired and paid for by the tenant. The tenant should, therefore, ensure that the insured risks stated are as wide as possible and should also include a general sweeper up. While the landlord himself has a vested interest in ensuring adequate insurance is in place, if for any reason the policy is faulty or certain standard commercial risks are not covered, the amendment proposed will ensure that the responsibility will not be the tenant's but will lie with the landlord. Specialist insurance advice may be needed by the tenant if *terrorism* and/or *explosion* is not a specifically stated risk. If it is not a stated risk and, for whatever reason, the landlord cannot be persuaded to cover terrorism as a specified risk it is important to ensure that, where appropriate, eg, the tenant's repairing obligation is amended to ensure that the tenant does not have to cover the cost of any damage occasioned by such an act. As the tenant is in fact paying for the insurance then, provided his requested amendments are sustainable and reasonable, there is no good reason for the landlord to refuse them.

1.19 If the interest rate stated in clause 1.20 ceases to exist for any reason (and who knows how many more banks are going to amalgamate?) then any alternative *interest rate* quoted by the landlord should be something reasonably comparable and not a punitive interest rate linked to some foreign or offshore institution. The proposed amendment caters for this.

1.20 The same principles apply here as those referred to above in relation to clause 1.19. The rate of interest at 5% (as originally drafted) is too high and punitive. By amending to 2% the hope is that a compromise of 3% or 4% will be agreed. If a landlord resists he should be told that he is receving money 'in advance' and will therefore earn money on it. See also clause 3.17 (Interest on arrears). It is important to ensure any provision in this clause is consistent with clause 3.17.

1.22 This is, arguably, one of the most important amendments that the tenant can make. For some time, based on the decision in *Finchbourne Ltd v Rodrigues* [1976] 3 All ER 581, CA, there was a view that a term would be implied into a lease that service charge expenditure could only be recovered by a landlord to the extent that it was reasonable. In two more recent cases, however, dealing with the recovery of insurance premiums, the courts have refused to imply such a limitation. The two cases are

1.23 'Liability Period'

(i) in the case of [*name of guarantor for Original Tenant*] the period during which the Original Tenant is bound by the tenant covenants of this Lease ~~together with any additional period during which the Original Tenant is liable under an authorised guarantee agreement~~

(ii) in the case of any guarantor required pursuant to subclause 3.9.5.2 of clause 3.9.5 CONDITIONS, the period during which the relevant assignee is bound by the tenant covenants of this Lease ~~together with any additional period during which that assignee is liable under an authorised guarantee agreement~~

(iii) in the case of any guarantor under an authorised guarantee agreement, the period during which the relevant assignee is bound by the tenant covenants of this Lease and

(iv) in the case of any guarantor required pursuant to subclause 3.9.8.7 of clause 3.9.8 TERMS OF A PERMITTED SUBLEASE, the period during which the relevant assignee of the sublease is bound by the tenant covenants of that sublease.

1.24 'Losses'

References to 'losses' are references to all reasonably foreseeable liabilities, damages or losses, awards of damages or compensation, penalties, costs, disbursements or expenses arising from any claim, demand, action or proceedings

1.25 '1954 Act'

the Landlord and Tenant Act 1954 and all statutes, regulations and orders included by virtue of clause 1.46.5 REFERENCES TO STATUTES

1.26 '1995 Act'

the Landlord and Tenant (Covenants) Act 1995 and all statutes, regulations and orders included by virtue of clause 1.46.5 REFERENCES TO STATUTES

1.27 'Office Covenants'

the covenants set out in Schedule 5 THE OFFICE COVENANTS

1.28 'Other buildings'

References to 'other buildings' are references to all the buildings now or at any time during the Term erected on any adjoining property of the Landlord

Bandar Property Holdings Ltd v JS Darwen (Successors) Ltd [1968] 2 All ER 305 and *Havenridge Ltd v Boston Dyers Ltd* [1994] 2 EGLR 73, CA. The only qualification that the courts imposed in both cases was that the expenditure must not be exorbitant. As the landlords in these cases had settled their premium in the ordinary course of their business, at arm's length and with a reputable insurer, it could not be called into question. The landlord is under no obligation to approach more than one insurer. Inclusion of these words will ensure that your tenant client does not become a test case in determining to resolve whether any such implied term exists in the situation where your client's landlord seeks to be unreasonable in the expenses he claims through the service charge!

1.23(i) There is currently a healthy debate as to whether or not the guarantor of an original tenant to the lease or the guarantor of any subsequent assignee of the lease can be required, pursuant to the Landlord and Tenant (Covenants) Act 1995, to stand as guarantor to that party when that party himself is, effectively, required to act as a guarantor pursuant to an Authorised Guarantee Agreement. Until the courts are called upon to make a ruling on this point, the guarantor's advisers are best placed to deal with this specifically in the documentation by excluding liability during any such period. The author's view is that any attempt by landlords to require sureties to guarantee an authorised guarantee agreement is likely to fall foul of the anti-avoidance provision contained in section 25 of the Landlord and Tenant (Covenants) Act 1995 but the debate rumbles on. There are certainly many well-respected practitioners who argue that such a requirement can be imposed and so from the tenant or guarantor's point of view it is better not to leave it to chance but to deal with it specifically.

1.23(ii) The same points apply here as those referred to above in relation to clause 1.23(i).

1.24 It is important that the tenant tries to limit any losses for which the landlord will seek to make him responsible to those recognised by the general law. The test laid down in *Hadley v Baxendale* (1854) 9 Exch 341 sets down the principle relating to remoteness of damage and the amendment seeks to reflect this.

1.29	**'Parking Bays'**	those areas of the Building allocated as parking bays
~~**1.30**~~	~~**'Permitted Hours'**~~	~~the period from 9.00 am to 6.00 pm Monday to Friday~~
1.30	**'Permitted Part'**	[the entirety of]/[that part of] the [ ]floor of the Premises
1.31	**'Plan'**	the plan or plans annexed to this Lease and numbered as appropriate
1.32	**'Planning Acts'**	the Town and Country Planning Act 1990 and all statutes, regulations and orders included by virtue of clause 1.46.5 REFERENCES TO STATUTES
1.33	**'Premises'**	the first and second floors and part of the third floor of the Building shown for the purposes of identification only edged red on ~~the~~ Plans 2, 3 and 4 and the Included Parking Bays and as more particularly defined in schedule 1 THE PREMISES
1.34	**'Rent'**	Until the First Review Date 'the Rent' means the Initial Rent. Thereafter 'the Rent' means the sum ascertained in accordance with schedule 4 THE RENT AND RENT REVIEW. 'The Rent' does not include the Insurance Rent, but the term 'the Lease Rents' means both the Rent and the Insurance Rent
1.35	**'Rent Commencement Date'**	[ ]
1.36	**'Retained Parts'**	the parts of the Building that are not let or constructed or adapted for letting, including, without prejudice to the generality of the foregoing, such parts of the main structure, walls, foundations and roofs of the Building as are not included in the Premises and would not be included in premises demised by leases of other units in the Building if let on the same terms as this Lease, and also including office accommodation for the estate manager and any ancillary staff
1.37	**'Review Dates'**	'The First Review Date' means [ ] 'The Review Dates' means the First Review Date and every [5th] anniversary of that date during the Contractual Term and any other date from time to time specified under Schedule 4, para 3.4 EFFECT OF COUNTER-INFLATION PROVISIONS. References to 'a review date' are reference to any one of the Review Dates

1.30 (new) While this proposed amendment will not always be relevant, in the context of this particular specimen lease (where the premises comprise two entire floors and part of another floor of an office building), it may be perfectly logical, and commercial good sense, that the tenant would want to sub-let a clearly defined part, ie the whole of any floor or the entire floor area that it has on a particular floor where the floor area does not comprise the entire floor. This will be dealt with in more detail later under the alienation provisions (see clause 3.9). The deletion of *Permitted Hours* from the original drafting simply seeks to give the tenant maximum flexibility. Whether this is possible clearly depends on the landlord's management of the building but it is certainly a question the tenant's adviser should be asking.

1.31 Accurate plans help to avoid dispute. Professionally drawn up and identified plans lessen this likelihood even further. The landlord should be requested to prepare accurate plans, ideally identified by a reference number.

1.35 This will often be left blank in the initial draft submitted by the landlord. The heads of terms must be checked to see if any rent free period has been negotiated and if they make no reference to a rent free period then it is, in the author's view, incumbent on the tenant's adviser to check with his client as to whether or not the issue has been raised *especially* if the tenant has or is likely to incur fit out costs in making the premises fit for his intended use.

1.36 As drafted this clause is probably acceptable from the tenant's point of view. It ensures that tenants or occupiers of let units do not end up paying the service charge for unlet units thereby, effectively, subsidising such units. If the definition does not make this absolutely clear, it would need amendment to reflect this. The critical words are '*...not let or constructed or adapted for letting...*'. If those words are not referred to in the definition, they should be put in.

1.37 As originally drafted, this clause by virtue of the definition of '*the Term*' (which includes any holding-over or statutory continuation tenancy (see clause 1.43)) enables the landlord to implement what is known as a 'penultimate day' rent review, although in reality this date may be the first day of any holding-over period where the tenant remains in occupation pursuant to the Landlord and Tenant Act 1954 sections [ ]. The

1.38	**'Service Charge'**	the Service Charge Percentage of the Landlord's Expenses.
1.39	**'Service Charge Percentage'**	[ ]% subject to the provisions for variation contained in Schedule 6 clause 2.6 VARIATION OF THE SERVICE CHARGE PERCENTAGE.
1.40	**'Services'**	the services, facilities and amenities specified in Schedule 6 clause 2.11 THE SERVICES
1.41	**'Surveyor'**	[ ] or any person who is or firm the majority of whose partners are, Fellows or Associates of the Royal Institution of Chartered Surveyors [or Associates or Fellows of the Incorporated Society of Valuers and Auctioneers] appointed by the Landlord in his place. The Surveyor may be an employee of the Landlord or a Group Company. The expression 'the Surveyor' includes the person or firm appointed by the Landlord to collect the Lease Rents
1.42	**'Tenant'**	includes any person who is for the time being bound by the tenant covenants of this Lease.
1.43	**'Term'**	the Contractual Term [and any period of holding-over or extension or continuance of the Contractual Term by statute or common law]
1.44	**'this Lease'**	Unless expressly stated to the contrary, the expression 'this Lease' includes any document stated to be supplemental to or collateral with this document or entered into in accordance with this document
1.45	**'VAT'**	value added tax ~~or any other tax of a similar nature~~ and, unless otherwise expressly stated, all references to rents or other sums payable by the Tenant are exclusive of VAT

amendment ensures that this will not happen. Landlords recognise that there may be a considerable gap between the expiry of the contractual term granted by the lease and the date on which the statutory tenancy ultimately comes to an end. Landlords will argue that by holding over under a statutory tenancy, the tenant may benefit from a historic low rent for as long as possible. The tenant should argue, however, against a penultimate day rent review on the ground that statute provides adequate protection for the landlord by virtue of the interim rent mechanism introduced by section 24A of the Landlord and Tenant Act 1954. This enables the landlord to make an application to the court for an interim rent to be paid. The practical procedural steps that apply to an interim rent application and the basis on which an interim rent is fixed are outside the scope of this book but the mechanism is there to ensure that the landlord gets a proper return during this period of holding over by the tenant. The tenant's adviser should therefore strenuously resist any attempts by the landlord to implement a penultimate day rent review.

1.39 The same comments apply here as those suggested in relation to clause 1.17.

1.41 The same principles referred to in clause 1.1 apply here. Depending on the nature and complexity of the building of which the premises form part and the likely management involvement associated with it, it is suggested that the stated professional criteria will give the tenant the additional comfort that any surveying duties should be carried out properly.

1.43 The square brackets have been incorporated here as a reminder that if the lease is *contracted out* from the security of tenure provisions granted by Part II of the Landlord and Tenant Act 1954 the words between them need to be deleted. It is also vitally important to consider the impact of the words in brackets on an original tenant (or assignee) under a pre-1 January 1996 Lease when the original tenant or assignee is no longer the tenant at the expiry of the contractual term. If the present tenant 'holds over' the original tenant's liability expires at the end of the contractual term (as does that of any assignee no longer the present tenant) <u>only</u> if the wording in brackets is <u>not</u> included or this liability is specifically excluded elsewhere (*City of London Corpn v Fell* [1994] 1 AC 458, HL).

1.44 This amendment is self-explanatory. The tenant would not want to be subject to obligations, liabilities or other onerous provisions brought in by a document (for example a licence) which was not clearly expressed to be supplemental to the lease itself.

1.45 The words deleted are very vague and potentially expose a tenant to an additional unknown and unquantified liability. The landlord may well require reinstatement of this clause and this may be acceptable to a tenant provided such a tax simply replaced VAT and did not impose any additional liability.

1.46.1 Words importing one gender include all other genders; words importing the singular include the plural and vice versa and any reference to persons includes not only individuals but companies or other corporate bodies

1.46.2 The clause, paragraph and schedule headings and the table of contents do not form part of this document and are not to be taken into account in its construction or interpretation

1.46.3 Any reference in this document to a clause, subclause, paragraph, subparagraph or schedule without further designation is to be construed as a reference to the clause, subclause, paragraph or schedule to this document so numbered

1.46.4.1 References to any right of the Landlord to have access to the Premises are to be construed as extending to any head landlord or mortgagee of the Premises (where the headlease or mortgage grants such rights of access to the headlandlord or mortgagee) and to all persons authorised in writing by the Landlord (or any head landlord or mortgagee having rights of access) including agents, professional advisers, contractors, workmen and others

1.46.4.2 References to any rights exercisable by the Tenant shall be construed as being exercisable by the Tenant, any sub-tenant or sub-tenants and all persons properly authorised by them

1.46.5 Unless expressly stated to the contrary any references to a specific statute include (save where in consequence of the same any additional or more onerous liability may be imposed on the Tenant or Guarantor) any statutory extension or modification, amendment or re-enactment of that statute and any regulations or orders made under that statute, and any general reference to a statute includes any regulations or orders made under that statute

1.47 Terms from the 1995 Act

Where the expressions 'landlord covenants', 'tenant covenants', or 'authorised guarantee agreement' are used in this Lease they are to have the meaning given by the 1995 Act section 28(1)

1.48 Interpretation of consent and approved

1.48.1 Prior written consent or approval

References to 'consent of the Landlord' or words to similar effect are references to a prior written consent signed by ~~or on behalf of~~ the Landlord and references to the need for anything to be 'approved by the Landlord' or words to similar effect are references to the need for a prior written approval by ~~or on behalf of~~ the Landlord

1.46.1 This amendment is self-explanatory.

1.46.2 This new clause is a mirror of clause 1.46.4.1 and is self-explanatory, ensuring there is no question mark over derivative parties' exercise of any rights granted in this lease to the tenant.

1.46.4 This amendment is self-explanatory. These additional words should be included so that the clause applies only where the consent of a mortgagee or head landlord is required under the terms of a mortgage or head lease that has been created before the lease is entered into. In addition to this, the prudent tenant should request a copy of the relevant document to ascertain if the rights of the mortgagor or head landlord do, in fact, exist. Unless these words are included the landlord could, by subsequently creating a mortgage or a head lease, bring about a situation where consent could be refused in circumstances in which it would otherwise have been unreasonable so to do. The need for mortgagee's or head landlord's consent is particularly relevant in the context of alienation where the effect on the tenant's ability to assign or sublet could be adverse to the tenant's interest at the date of the lease.

1.46.5 The proposed amendment here seeks to draw a line in the sand so that the tenant's liability is established at the commencement of the lease for the duration of the term and is not subsequently increased following statutory or other legislative changes during the lifetime of the lease. This is unlikely to prove acceptable to the landlord but nonetheless the tenant may consider it appropriate to raise the issue.

1.48.1 The last thing that a tenant needs is a dispute as to whether or not a person or party signing any form of consent or approval has the relevant authority to do so. The amendment seeks to avoid this.

1.48.2 Consent or approval of mortgagee or head landlord

Any provisions in this Lease referring to the consent or approval of the Landlord are to be construed as also requiring the consent or approval of any mortgagee of the Premises and any head landlord, where that consent is required under the terms of a mortgage or headlease in existence at the date of this Lease. Nothing in this Lease is to be construed as imposing any obligation on a mortgagee or head landlord not to refuse any consent or approval unreasonably

1.48.3 References to 'the last year of the Term' are references to the actual last year of the Term howsoever it determines, and references to the 'end of the Term' are references to the end of the Term whensoever and howsoever it determines

1.49 Joint and several liability

Where any party to this Lease for the time being comprises two or more persons, obligations expressed or implied to be made by or with that party are deemed to be made by or with the persons comprising that party jointly and severally

1.50 Obligation not to permit or suffer

Any covenant by the Tenant not to do anything includes an obligation not to knowingly permit or knowingly suffer that thing to be done by another person

1.51 Interpretation of 'the Premises'

In the absence of any provision to the contrary, references to 'the Premises' include any part of the Premises

2 DEMISE

2.1 The Landlord demises the Premises to the Tenant together with the rights specified in Schedule 2 THE RIGHTS GRANTED but excepting and reserving to the Landlord the rights specified in Schedule 3 THE RIGHTS RESERVED, to hold to the Tenant for the Contractual Term subject to ~~all rights, easements, privileges, restrictions, covenants and stipulations of whatever nature affecting the Premises including any~~ those matters contained or referred to in Schedule 2 THE SUBJECTIONS yielding and paying to the Landlord:

2.1.1 the Rent, ~~without any deduction or set-off,~~ by equal quarterly payments in advance on the usual quarter days in every year and proportionately for any period of less than a year, the first such payment, being a proportionate sum in respect of the period from and including the Rent Commencement Date to and including the day before the quarter day next after the Rent Commencement Date, [to be paid on the date of this document] and

1.48.2 The same arguments apply here as those referred to in clause 1.46.4 above.

1.49 Sometimes this clause will not, intentionally on the part of the landlord, make reference to the landlord. It should be amended to ensure it refers to <u>all</u> parties to the lease.

1.50 This additional word '*knowingly*' is wonderfully effective for the tenant. Landlords may be hard pushed to argue that a tenant should be responsible for something he knows nothing about and may accept that the tenant should not be under strict liability. While the relative bargaining strengths will be all important (as ever) the tenant should press strongly for such an amendment.

DEMISE

2.1 The tenant would be ill-advised to enter into a lease without knowing what encumbrances affect the premises at the time he takes the lease. These should be clearly set out in a schedule. The general wording which has been deleted is far too wide ranging and, in the author's view, absolutely unacceptable. As the landlord is not obliged to deduce title (but he can, of course, always be asked to do so and in some cases the tenant should insist) there may be provisions contained in the freehold title or a head lease which render the tenant's proposals for the premises not only unviable but illegal. If the landlord insists on such a provision as originally drafted, the tenant should insist that title is deduced. There is a strong arguable case that if the tenant has agreed to pay the landlord's legal costs in connection with the grant of the lease (see clause 3.27) then at the very least this additional work should be paid for by the landlord.

2.1.1 Deduction and set off are valuable weapons in the tenant's armoury and, while many landlords (particularly institutional landlords) insist on what have become known as *clear leases* (ie leases where they are guaranteed that every month or quarter they will receive their rent clear of any deductions), the author considers that there is no good reason why the rights of deduction or set off should be lost if the landlord is in breach of his contractual leasehold obligations. The tenant can argue that every provision in the lease which involves expenditure by the landlord is mirrored by a provision requiring the tenant to reimburse the landlord for such expenditure and this argument should be used to reinstate the right to deduction and set off. In any event there could be instances where the tenant must make deductions (eg if the landlord is based offshore and tax becomes payable directly to the Inland Revenue). As an absolute minimum, therefore, the words '*...(save where required by statute)...*' should be included.

2.1.2 by way of further rent the Service Charge payable in accordance with Schedule 6 THE SERVICE CHARGE and the Insurance Rent payable ~~on~~ within [21] days of demand in accordance with clause 5.4 PAYMENT OF THE INSURANCE RENT

3 THE TENANT'S COVENANTS

The Tenant covenants with the Landlord to observe and perform the requirements of this clause 3

3.1 Rent

3.1.1 Payment of the Lease Rents

The Tenant must pay the Lease Rents on the days and in the manner set out in this Lease~~, and must not exercise or seek to exercise any right or claim to withhold rent, or any right or claim to legal or equitable set-off~~

3.1.2 Payment by banker's order

If so reasonably required in writing by the Landlord, the Tenant must pay the Lease Rents by banker's order or credit transfer to any bank and account in the UK that the Landlord reasonably nominates from time to time

3.2 Outgoings and VAT

3.2.1 Outgoings exclusive to the Premises

The Tenant must pay, and must indemnify the Landlord against:

3.2.1.1 all rates, taxes, assessments, duties, charges, impositions and outgoings (save those of a capital nature) that are now or may at any time during the Term be charged, assessed or imposed on the Premises or on the ~~owner or~~ occupier of them (excluding any payable by the Landlord occasioned by receipt of the Lease Rents or by any

2.1.2 Periods of grace are not unusual and are generally commercially acceptable to landlords so that interest provisions do not immediately become operative. If this is common practice there is no reason why it should not be enshrined and become a contractual provision.

THE TENANT'S COVENANTS

3.1.1 Although the words '*...yielding and paying...*' referred to in clause 2.1 actually imply a covenant on the part of the tenant to pay the rent, a specific covenant is invariably included. As has been stated in relation to clause 2.1.1 the ability to *set off* is a valuable weapon in the tenant's limited armoury. Landlords, particularly institutional landlords, are always keen to have a *clean* lease, meaning that all rental due is received gross. However, there can be little compelling argument from the landlord's point of view as to why, if a tenant has to spend his own money complying with what is contractually a landlord's obligation, it should not have the right to set off (meaning it can deduct from the rent and other sums due to the landlord the cost of so complying). Landlords will no doubt argue that tenants have suitable remedies for breach of contract if the landlord is in breach but this involves the expense and delay of making a claim and potential litigation on the part of the tenant. The self-help remedy of *set off* is much more appealing from a tenant's point of view and should be argued for strongly. Landlords should be pressed for compelling reasons as to why this right should not be available.

3.1.2 If rental payments are made by banker's order (by agreement) then it is important that the tenant does what it can to ensure that his accounts department is not inadvertently notified to send money to an offshore account. If a request for offshore payments is received then such payments must be made net of basic rate tax. If rental payments are made gross (in error) then it is difficult, if not impossible, for the tenant to recover this tax element of the rent. The tenant would still, however, have to account to the Inland Revenue for the basic rate tax payments which means a double payment. The amendments to the clause seek to ensure this will not happen. One argument for deletion of this clause in its entirety is to make the landlord aware that acceptance of such a payment by a landlord could in certain circumstances amount to a waiver or tenant's breach of covenant. The author has often used this argument successfully as landlords view deletion of the clause as the lesser of two 'evils'.

3.2.1.1 A number of issues arise in relation to this clause. Firstly, on a shorter-term lease, the tenant should seek to ensure that any capital outgoings relating to the premises fall to be paid by the landlord. The tenant should not be seen to be funding *betterment* and giving the landlord back something more valuable than that which he granted. It is not easy to

disposition of or dealing with this Lease or ownership of any interest reversionary to the interest created by it)provided that if, after the end of the Term, the Landlord suffers loss of any rating relief applicable to empty premises because the relief has been allowed to the Tenant in respect of a period before the end of the Term, then the Tenant must make good such loss to the Landlord

3.2.1.2 all VAT from time to time charged on the Lease Rents or other sums payable by the Tenant under this Lease provided that the Landlord shall have previously delivered to the Tenant a valid VAT invoice addressed to the Tenant for the full amount

3.2.1.3 all VAT incurred in relation to any costs that the Tenant is obliged to pay or in respect of which he is required to indemnify the Landlord under the terms of this Lease provided that the Landlord shall have previously delivered to the Tenant a valid VAT invoice addressed to the Tenant for the full amount

3.2.2 Outgoings assessed on the Premises and other property

The Tenant must pay, and must indemnify the Landlord against, the proportion reasonably attributable to the Premises (to be determined from time to time by the Surveyor, acting as an expert and not as an arbitrator) of all rates, taxes, assessments, duties, charges, impositions and outgoings save those of a capital nature that are now or at any time during the Term may be charged, assessed or imposed on the Premises and any other property, including the rest of the Building any adjoining property of the Landlord, or on the owner or occupier of them and it

3.3 Cost of services consumed

The Tenant must pay to the suppliers, and indemnify the Landlord against, all charges for electricity, water, gas, telecommunications and other services consumed or used by the Tenant at or in relation to the Premises, including meter rents and standing charges, and must comply with the lawful requirements and regulations of the respective suppliers of which the Tenant has received written notice

identify when a shorter-term lease becomes a longer-term lease such that a tenant could be reasonably expected to be responsible for outgoings of a capital nature, but the author would suggest that anything over a 5- or 6-year term may well fall into this latter category. Secondly, it is essential that a tenant ensures that any corporation tax or income tax payable by the landlord as a result of the receipt of the rent or any other payments due under the lease similarly fall to be paid by the landlord. Thirdly, any taxes falling due on the landlord's dealings with any interest in reversion to the lease again should be payable by the landlord. As a final point, the tenant should delete reference to the loss of rating relief. If the landlord gives up control of the property to the tenant for the term created by the lease then if, in the commercial interests of the tenant, the tenant decides to vacate the premises and obtains rating relief, there is no reason why he should be penalised for this by having to reimburse the landlord on expiry of the lease.

3.2.1.2 Current VAT legislation states that the provider of a service must provide a valid VAT invoice in relation to any input tax incurred by the paying party. All too often difficulties are encountered with VAT invoices not being available at the time payments are made and often they never materialise. This is particularly relevant when premiums are paid on assignments of leases. The tenant's (or assignee's) solicitor must ensure that such an invoice is available before or at the time payment is made. The only bargaining stick which the tenant has is to be able to say that he is not going to meet the payment until the invoice is available. Once the payment has been made there is no incentive for the landlord to provide the invoice.

3.2.1.3 Exactly the same comments apply here as in clause 3.2.1.2 above.

3.2.2 The same point can be made here concerning outgoings of a capital nature as has been made in relation to clause 3.2.1.1 above. The tenant has the protection, if the tenant's adviser has made the appropriate amendments to the draft lease (see clause 1.41), of knowing that the surveyor will act in an ethical and proper manner. The addition of the word *reasonably* further enforces this obligation.

3.3 It is unlikely that anyone other than the tenant will have used the services but just in case there is a question mark over consumption, for example, of water, this amendment at least gives the tenant a chance to argue with the landlord. The second amendment is self-explanatory. The tenant cannot be expected to comply with issues of which he is not aware. While as occupier he is very likely to have been notified by the suppliers, sometimes, inadvertently, freeholders can be contacted directly by statutory undertakers and other service providers, and the second amendment is designed to ensure that any such information received by the landlord is passed onto the tenant.

3.4 Repair, cleaning and decoration

3.4.1 Repair of the Premises

The Tenant must repair the Premises and keep them in good condition and repair, damages by an Insured Risk, acts of terrorism or structural or inherent defects excepted, PROVIDED ALWAYS the Tenant shall not be obliged by this or any other obligation contained anywhere in this Lease to put the Premises into any better state of repair and condition than that evidenced by the Schedule of Condition attached hereto and initialled by or on behalf of the parties to this Lease

3.4.1 This clause has been drafted originally as a standard tenant's full repairing obligation. There may be compelling reasons why, in the circumstances of the letting in question, this is not appropriate, eg a short-term letting or a letting of a dilapidated building. In the context of the lease we are considering (a lease of a suite of offices comprising only a part of a building), this repairing obligation relates only to the interior of the premises. If it is not appropriate for whatever reason to have a tenant's full repairing obligation (because, for example, the windows are in need of replacement or the central heating is archaic), the amendment suggested is an obvious way to mitigate the harshness of such a clause on the tenant. The only downside to this amendment is that it does involve the preparation of a schedule of condition at additional cost. As the tenant is the one likely to be requesting such a schedule the landlord may well turn the argument around and say that if the tenant wants a schedule of condition he must pay for it. However, in the context of potential dilapidation claims during or at the end of the term, a few hundred pounds paid to a surveyor to prepare such a schedule may well be money well spent and a very useful insurance policy. The schedule will usually comprise a portfolio of photographs with a written commentary or, in other instances, may be undertaken on a video camera with a narrative. It is essential that whichever method is adopted a final product is agreed with the landlord. There should be little room for dispute as it should merely be a record of factual matters. It is a question of fact and degree and a consideration of all the circumstances, in particular the state of the building and the nature of the services, which will dictate whether or not the tenant tries to push matters further and provide that he is not responsible, via the service charge, for repairs and/or improvements to the building of which the particular demised premises form part. This is likely to prove less attractive to the landlord but a tenant should, nevertheless, attempt to mitigate the potential harshness of having to contribute large sums via the service charge to, for example, repairing or improving the structure of the building. (See clauses 6.2.8 and 6.2.11.1 under Schedule 6). Other matters which will need specific consideration in the context of both the repairing clause and the extent to which a tenant must contribute to repairs via the service charge are terrorism and structural and inherent defects. The author would always suggest that disrepair due to terrorism (whether insured against or not) should be excluded specifically from both the tenant's repairing covenant and also the service charge heads of expenditure, while disrepair which manifests itself as a result of inherent or structural defect is more a matter of negotiation. Collateral warranties may be available to an original tenant of new-built premises which would mitigate the hardship of the repairs in such circumstances, but a tenant would still then need to prove negligence on the part of the professionals involved in the design and construction of the premises. An alternative would be to accept an obligation from the landlord and its successor (by way of a covenant) to pursue the professionals in an action for negligence under their Letters of Appointment or building contract. Ideally the tenant would want no liability for disrepair arising from any such manifestation. It is much better to exclude it in its entirety.

3.4.2 Replacement of landlord's fixtures

The Tenant must replace any landlord's fixtures and fittings in the Premises that are beyond economic repair~~ at any time during or~~ at the end of the Term

3.4.3 Cleaning and tidying

The Tenant must keep the Premises clean and tidy and clear of all rubbish

3.4.4 The Included Parking Bays

3.4.4.1 Care of the Included Parking Bays

The Tenant must ~~keep the Included Parking Bays adequately marked out, surfaced, in good condition and free from weeds, and must~~ use them for car parking only

3.4.4.2 Storage on the Included Parking Bays

The Tenant must not store anything on the Included Parking Bays or bring anything onto them that is likely to cause a legal nuisance~~is or might become untidy, unclean, unsightly or in any way detrimental to the Building or the area generally~~

3.4.4.3 Rubbish on the Included Parking Bays

The Tenant must not deposit any waste, rubbish or refuse on the Included Parking Bays or place any receptacle for waste, rubbish or refuse on them

3.4.4.4 Caravans on the Included Parking Bays

The Tenant must not keep or store any caravan or movable dwelling on the Included Parking Bays

3.4.5 Decoration

The Tenant must redecorate the Premises in a good and workmanlike manner, with appropriate materials of good quality, and to the reasonable satisfaction of the Surveyor in each of the Decorating Years and in the last year of the Term, any change in the tints, colours and patterns of the decoration to be approved by the Landlord (such approval not to be unreasonably withheld or delayed) PROVIDED ALWAYS that the Tenant shall not be obliged by this or any other provision in this Lease to decorate the Premises more than once in any [three (3)] year period

3.4.2 This amendment is self-explanatory. The tenant should have obtained, through the replies to his preliminary enquiries, a full listing of what the landlord considers to be his fixtures and fittings at the premises so the tenant knows *exactly* what such obligations relate to. There is a point when repairs become economically unviable and the only real alternative is replacement. This amendment attempts to give the tenant as much scope as possible to go down the cheaper route.

3.4.4.1 The deletion here is intended only when the lease is for a shorter term (see clause 3.2). With a shorter-term letting a tenant will not want the expense of having to undertake the works referred to in the clause as originally drawn. Again, much will depend on the individual facts of each particular letting but on a short-term letting these requirements are unduly onerous. It is important to bear in mind that if car parking bays in a somewhat dilapidated state are actually included in the definition of the premises, photographs or video footage of the bays should be included in a schedule of condition to ensure that any repair costs do not fall on the tenant.

3.4.4.2 The proposed amendment is intended to spell out contractually what can and cannot be done. The deleted words are very subjective and will mean different things to different people. The amendment attempts to put on a legal footing those things that the tenant cannot do by reference to the tort of nuisance. While a court would have to decide what is or might be untidy, unclean, unsightly or in any way detrimental to the building or the area generally if the matter was litigated, the author suspects that this is an area fraught with potential conflicting views by the parties and that such widely subjective provisions are best avoided.

3.4.5 The first amendment is designed to ensure that the landlord is not unreasonable in its decorative requirements while the second attempts to ensure, particularly towards the end of the term, that the obligation to decorate is not unduly onerous by requiring it to be done more than once in such a short period of time that the second set of decorations are not, in the circumstances, really required. The author has stated as long a period as possible which is likely to prove acceptable to the landlord, but it may well be that the landlord would attempt to negotiate the period down.

3.5 Waste and alterations

3.5.1 Waste, additions and alterations

The Tenant must not commit any waste, make any addition to the Premises, unite the Premises with any adjoining premises, or make any structural alteration to the Premises except as permitted by the provisions of this clause 3.5

3.5.2 Preconditions for alterations

The Tenant must not make any structural alterations to the Premises unless he first:

3.5.2.1 obtains and complies with the necessary consents of the competent authorities and pays their charges for them

3.5.2.2 makes an application to the Landlord for consent, supported by reasonable drawings and where appropriate a reasonable specification in duplicate ~~prepared by an architect, or a member of some other appropriate profession, who must supervise the work throughout to completion~~

3.5.2.3 pays the reasonable and proper fees of the Landlord (and where required by any headlease or mortgage), any head landlord, any mortgagee and their respective professional advisers

3.5.2.4 enters into any reasonable covenants the Landlord reasonably requires as to the execution and reinstatement of the alterations and

3.5.2.5 obtains the consent of the Landlord such consent not to be unreasonably withheld or delayed

In the case of any works of a substantial nature, the Landlord may where circumstances might reasonably require it require the Tenant to provide, before starting the works, ~~adequate~~ reasonable security in the form of a deposit of money or the provision of a bond as assurance to the Landlord that any works he permits from time to time will be fully completed.

3.5.1 Waste is very widely defined in legal terms and includes voluntary waste, permissive waste, ameliorative waste and equitable waste (topics beyond the scope of this book). In practice demolition and alterations to buildings will often amount to be waste. The likelihood of the tenant wanting to make alterations to any particular premises is always going to be a question of fact and degree and therefore accepting an absolute prohibition on alteration is not advisable. If a qualified prohibition is included it is important that the tenant realises that (unless the alteration constitutes 'an improvement') there is no statutorily implied term which states that such consent cannot unreasonably be withheld. In a letting such as this (office space) there is always going to be the likelihood of the tenant wanting to put up and take down internal de-mountable stud partitioning walls to make the best use of the available space (see new clause 3.5.3). Every time the tenant wishes to do this, he does not want to have to go to the landlord for formal consent with the cost and delays associated with such applications. When the landlord is letting an area of office space (as in this circumstance), there is no detriment to the landlord if the internal partitions are being moved around providing that if *reasonably* required at the end of the term, the tenant is under an obligation to give the landlord back the premises in the state in which he took them. Structural alterations are, however, a completely different matter and it is perfectly reasonable for a landlord to exercise a high degree of control over such structural alterations. The amendment to clause 3.5.1 attempts to reflect this.

3.5.2.2 The amendments to this clause are designed to minimise the cost to the tenant so far as possible. It may not be necessary, in the context to the proposed works, for the drawings and specification to be prepared by an architect or other professionally qualified person. Inclusion of the word '*reasonable*', twice, gives the landlord the necessary protection.

3.5.2.3 The fetter on fees is self-explanatory. The second amendment ensures that the tenant is able, at the time he enters into the lease, to know the extent of the obligations he has in relation to the cost of obtaining consent from any head landlord or mortgagee.

3.5.2.4 The amendments here are intended to ensure that the tenant is not held to ransom by the landlord in relation to the proposed alterations. If the landlord can sustain reasonable arguments with reasonable reasons as to why the alterations should be undertaken in a particular way or why there should be reinstatement, the tenant is likely to have little choice but to accept these; but the tenant should not be at the whim of the landlord in this respect.

3.5.2.5 This amendment which is self-explanatory and is an important one because without it a landlord may frustrate a tenant by not responding at all or by acting in a dilatory fashion. The amendment to the final paragraph of the clause seeks simply to introduce, once again, an element of fairness into the conduct of the landlord.

3.5.3 Internal partitions

Without prejudice to the provisions of this clause 3.5, the Tenant may install and remove internal demountable partitions if he gives notice of the works to the Landlord within one month of completion of the works and ensures that there is no disruption of the services in, to and through the Premises

~~**3.5.3 Removal of alterations**~~

~~At the end of the Term, if so requested by the Landlord, the Tenant must remove any additions, alterations or improvements made to the Premises, and must make good any loss occasioned by such removal~~

3.5.4 Connection to the Conduits

The Tenant must not make any connection with the Conduits that serve the Premises without the Landlord's consent such consent not to be unreasonably withheld or delayed

3.6 Aerials signs and advertisements

3.6.1 Masts and wires

The Tenant must not erect any pole or mast or install any cable or wire on the Premises, whether in connection with telecommunications or otherwise without the Landlord's consent such consent not to be unreasonably withheld or delayed

3.6.2 Advertisements

The Tenant must not fix to or exhibit on the outside of the Premises, or fix to or exhibit through any window of the Premises, or display anywhere on the Premises any placard, sign, notice, fascia, board or advertisement, except, with the consent of the Landlord such consent not to be unreasonably withheld or delayed, a sign of the same design, so far as possible, as those the Tenant has the right, by virtue of Schedule 2 clause 3 DISPLAY OF NAMEPLATES OR SIGNS, to have displayed on the outside of the Building and in the reception area of the Building PROVIDED ALWAYS that nothing in this subclause or in any other provision of this Lease shall preclude the Tenant from displaying its usual trade or corporate logo as aforesaid

3.7 Statutory obligations

3.7.1 General provision

To the extent that compliance is not the obligation of the Landlord pursuant to his obligations contained in this Lease or under the general

3.5.3 (new) As explained at clause 3.5.1, this new clause seeks to differentiate between alterations of a structural and non-structural nature by ensuring that a tenant can install and remove partitioning without requiring the prior consent of the landlord. The final part of the clause should give the landlord all the protection he needs.

3.5.3 Deletion of this clause is designed to ensure that any alterations undertaken and the requirement for reinstatement are considered on their own merits at the time consent for them is sought by the tenant. It is unlikely to prove acceptable to the landlord.

3.5.4 This amendment is simply designed to translate an absolute prohibition into a qualified prohibition. There are often no compelling reasons at the outset of a transaction why there should be an absolute prohibition on the tenant from doing certain things on the premises which will not adversely affect the value of the landlord's reversion. A qualified prohibition will almost always give the landlord the necessary protection because if what is proposed is likely to damage the value of his reversion or, in any other way, cause him difficulty he is entitled to refuse consent. An absolute prohibition, on the other hand from the tenant's perspective, gives the tenant absolutely no room for manoeuvre and should, when appropriate, be strenuously resisted.

3.6.1 Exactly the same point can be made here as under clause 3.5.4.

3.6.2 The first amendment again changes the obligation from an absolute prohibition to a qualified prohibition while the proviso at the end of the clause provides that any nationally recognised or instantly recognisable trade or corporate logos are not subject to any such control. If the landlord has been negotiating to grant a lease to a party who has such trade logos it is reasonably safe to assume that part of the attraction from the landlord's point of view is likely to be the strength of the covenant associated with that body.

3.7.1 The first amendment ensures that liability for compliance is accepted by the landlord where either he has freely accepted it in the lease or by virtue of the general law, while the words in brackets should be included

law [and save where the same involves capital expenditure] the Tenant must comply in all respects with the requirements of any statutes applicable to the use by the Tenant of the Premises or the trade or business for the time being carried on there and any other obligations so applicable imposed by law or by any byelaws

3.7.2 Particular obligations

3.7.2.1 Works required by statute, department or authority

Without prejudice to the generality of clause 3.7.1, the Tenant must execute all works and provide and maintain all arrangements on or in respect of ~~the Premises or~~ the use to which the Premises are being put that are required in order to comply with the requirements of any statute already ~~or in the future to be~~ passed, or the requirements of any government department, local authority or other public or competent authority or court of competent jurisdiction~~, regardless of whether such requirements are imposed on the owner, the occupier, or any other person~~

3.7.2.2 Acts causing losses

Without prejudice to the generality of clause 3.7.1, the Tenant must not knowingly do in or near the Premises anything by reason of which the Landlord may incur any losses under any statute

3.7.2.3 Construction (Design and Management) Regulations

Without prejudice to the generality of clause 3.7.1, the Tenant must insofar as they relate to any works the tenant may undertake comply with the provisions of the Construction (Design and Management) Regulations 1994 ('the CDM Regulations'), be the only client as defined in the provisions of the CDM Regulations, fulfil in relation to all and any works all the obligations of the client as set out in or reasonably to be inferred from the CDM Regulations, and make a declaration to that effect to the Health and Safety Executive in accordance with the Approved Code of Practice published from time to time by the Health and Safety Executive in relation to the CDM Regulations. The provisions of clause 5.7.3 FIRE-FIGHTING EQUIPMENT are to have effect in any circumstances to which these obligations apply

3.7.2.4 Delivery of health and safety files

At the end of the Term, the Tenant must ~~forthwith~~ as soon as reasonably practicable deliver to the Landlord any and all health and safety files relating to the premises in accordance with the CDM Regulations

in a shorter-term lease to ensure the tenant is not paying to improve the value of the landlord's investment. The second amendment proposed here attempts to narrow down the tenant's liability so that it is only the tenant's actual presence and use of the building which gives rise to an obligation to comply with the statutes referred to. So far as the building itself is concerned, particularly in relation to shorter-term lettings, this clause as drafted is an attempt by the landlord to shift the responsibility for compliance to the tenant. The amendment seeks to shift it back!

3.7.2.1 The first deletion in this particular clause merely attempts to reinforce the points made under clause 3.7.1 while the second attempts to ensure that the *extent* of the tenant's liability is fixed at the date of the lease and not extended by subsequent statutes or subordinate legislation. The final deletion seeks to reinforce the first of these points.

3.7.2.2 This clause imposes *strict liability* on the part of the tenant, and the tenant's adviser should try to introduce the element of knowledge and seek to ensure that his client is not unknowingly saddled with this liability. It is, in reality, very likely to be impossible to comply at all times during a lease term with all relevant statutes which relate to occupation of a building and few, if any, tenants are going to know the full extent of their statutory obligations.

3.7.2.3 The *Construction (Design and Management) Regulations 1994* apply in only a limited set of circumstances and in relation to particular works of construction and the detail is beyond the scope of this book. There is one argument for stating that this clause should be deleted in its entirety bearing in mind the wide provisions contained in clause 3.7.1 but the amendment here makes the provisions operative only in so far as they relate to any works the tenant may decide to undertake.

3.7.2.4 An obligation to do something *forthwith* is, in many circumstances, likely to prove impossible to comply with. The proposed amendment simply attempts to deal with the reality of this situation.

3.8 Entry to inspect and notice to repair

3.8.1 Entry and notice

Where the same cannot otherwise be undertaken Tthe Tenant must permit the Landlord (on reasonable prior written notice):

3.8.1.1 to enter the Premises to ascertain whether or not the covenants and conditions of this Lease have been observed and performed,

3.8.1.2 to view the state of repair and condition of the Premises and other parts of the Premises where that is necessary in order to do so the Landlord making good as soon as reasonably practicable any damage thereby caused when such opening up reveals no breaches, and

3.8.1.3 to give to the Tenant, or notwithstanding clause 8.6 NOTICES leave on the Premises, a notice ('a notice to repair') specifying the works required to remedy any breach of the Tenant's obligations in this Lease

3.8.2 Works to be carried out

The Tenant must commence carrying out the works specified in a notice to repair as soon as reasonably practicableimmediately, (including, making good any opening up) (but only where the opening up has revealed breaches)

3.8.3 Landlord's power in default

If within 1 month of the service of a notice to repair the Tenant has not started to execute the work referred to in that notice or is not proceeding diligently with it, or if the Tenant fails to finish the work as soon as reasonably practicable within 2 months or if in the Landlord's reasonable opinion the Tenant is unlikely to finish the work within that period, the Tenant must permit the Landlord to enter the Premises to execute the outstanding work, and must, on demand, pay to the Landlord the reasonable and proper cost of so doing and all expenses incurred by the Landlord, including legal costs and surveyor's fees as soon as reasonably practicable PROVIDED ALWAYS that any such costs which fall to be reimbursed by the Landlord shall not exceed any which would be recoverable by the Landlord pursuant to the relevant provision of the Leasehold Property (Repairs Act) 1938 and section 18(1) of the Landlord and Tenant Act 1927

3.9 Alienation

3.9.1 Alienation prohibited

The Tenant must not hold the Premises on trust for another. The Tenant must not part with possession of the Premises or any part of them or permit another to occupy them or any part of them except

3.8.1 The proposed amendment to this clause seeks to ensure that before entering the premises occupied by the tenant (and causing disruption and possible alarm amongst the tenant's employees - 'Why were the landlord's representatives crawling around the office yesterday?') the landlord has explored whether or not there is any alternative available to him before coming onto the premises. If this is absolutely necessary there should at least be some reasonable notice in order that the tenant can take the appropriate action, ie arrange for this to be done outside office hours or notifying staff that there is nothing to worry about and what the purpose of the inspection is.

3.8.1.2 Opening up floors could cause untold problems for a tenant and this should be forcibly resisted. If a landlord insists then he must accept that if the opening up reveals no breaches of covenant not only should he make good any physical damage he may have caused to the premises but if the tenant has suffered any financial loss, this too should be made good by the landlord. The risks associated may well serve as sufficient deterrent to the tenant. The amendment suggested achieves this.

3.8.2 The first two amendments here are self-explanatory and seek to give a tenant a little more scope as regards a timetable for commencing any necessary works while the final amendment seeks to ensure that if the landlord has opened up any part of the premises (which the tenant should most definitely try and resist) and no breaches have been revealed then the obligation to reinstate rests with the landlord and not the tenant.

3.8.3 The landlord's self-help remedy contained in this clause is not available unless specifically set out and therefore, ideally, the tenant's adviser should delete it! The clause has the effect of allowing the landlord to recover the costs of such works as a debt and it has the benefit (from the landlord's point of view) of avoiding the provisions of the Leasehold Property (Repairs) Act 1938 because the landlord's claim is for a debt and not damages. In addition and for the same reason the limitation imposed on the level of recoverable costs by section 18(1) of the Landlord and Tenant Act 1927 will not apply. These principles were confirmed in *Jervis v Harris* [1996] 1 All ER 303, CA. If the tenant does not succeed in having the clause deleted the amendments to the clause seek to ensure that the balance is as fair as possible in relation to works which are required. As the provision only operates when the tenant is in default a landlord will seek to argue that there should be no fetter on the costs that he incurs in exercising his self-help remedy but the tenant will be ill advised to accept an obligation effectively to present the landlord with a blank cheque. The proviso attempts to contractually incorporate the statutory provisions and nullify the clause's attempt to 'contract-out' of them.

pursuant to a transaction permitted by and effected in accordance with the provisions of this Lease

3.9.2 Assignment~~, subletting~~ and charging of part

The Tenant must not assign~~, sublet~~ or charge part only of the Premises.

3.9.3 Assignment of the whole

Subject to clauses 3.9.4 CIRCUMSTANCES and 3.9.5 CONDITIONS, the Tenant must not assign the whole of the Premises without the consent of the Landlord, whose consent may not be unreasonably withheld or delayed

3.9.4 Circumstances

If any of the following circumstances (which are specified for the purposes of the Landlord and Tenant Act 1927 section 19(1A)) applies either at the date when application for consent to assign is made to the Landlord, or after that date but before the Landlord's consent is given, the Landlord may withhold his consent and if, after the Landlord's consent has been given but before the assignment has taken place, any such circumstances apply, the Landlord may revoke his consent, ~~whether~~ where his consent is expressly subject to a condition as referred to in subclause 3.9.5.4~~ or not~~. The circumstances are:

3.9.4.1 that any undisputed and material sum due from the Tenant under this Lease remains unpaid

3.9.4.2 that in the Landlord's reasonable opinion the assignee is not a person who is likely to be able to comply with the tenant covenants of this Lease~~ and to continue to be able to comply with them following the assignment~~

3.9.4.3 that without prejudice to subclause 3.9.4.2, in the case of an assignment to a Group Company in the Landlord's reasonable opinion the assignee is a person who is, or may become, less likely to be able to comply with the tenant covenants of this Lease than the Tenant requesting consent to assign, which likelihood is to be adjudged by reference in particular to the financial strength of that Tenant ~~aggregated with that of any guarantor of the obligations of that Tenant~~ and the value of any other security for the performance of the tenant covenants of this Lease when assessed at the date of grant or (where that Tenant is not the Original Tenant) the date of the assignment of this Lease to that Tenant or

3.9.4.4 that the assignee or any guarantor for the assignee, other than any guarantor under an authorised guarantee agreement, is a corporation registered (or otherwise resident) in a jurisdiction in which the order of a court obtained in England and Wales will not necessarily be enforced against the assignee or guarantor without any consideration of the merits of the case

3.9.2 While stating the obvious that the tenant's adviser must always look at the particular circumstances of the letting and the needs of the tenant, the letting envisaged by our specimen lease is a classic example where there is likely to be merit in the tenant having the ability to sublet *part* of the premises. As the premises are arranged on three different levels it may well be possible to agree with the landlord, as a point of principle, that subletting either the whole of a particular floor or specified parts of each floor should be acceptable to the landlord. The amendment proposed seeks to cater for that eventuality.

3.9.3 There is a vast legal difference between *withholding* and *delaying* consents and while a tenant has statutory rights in such circumstances under the Landlord and Tenant Act 1988, the additional words seek to give the tenant some redress if the landlord delays.

3.9.4 This amendment is self-explanatory.

3.9.4.1 It may be that, at the time an application is made for the relevant licence to assign, a sum of money allegedly due from tenant to landlord is unpaid but the reason that it has not been paid by the tenant is that it is disputed. If there is a genuine dispute there is no reason why this should delay landlord's consent. In addition insignificant outstanding sums should not delay the giving of covenant.

3.9.4.2 The words which have been deleted here are very difficult to interpret, smack of crystal ball gazing and act in a most unfair way against the tenant and any possible assignee. There is always a possibility that at some time in the future an assignee is not going to be able to comply with the tenant's covenants in the lease irrespective of its initial covenant strength. Nothing in the future is *absolutely* guaranteed. The judgement as to whether an assignee is likely to be able to *currently* comply has to be made by the landlord at the time the application for consent is made.

3.9.4.3 The amendment here simply seeks to compare like with like. It will often be the case that the covenant strength of an original tenant aggregated with that of a guarantor is going to be greater than that of a potential assignee alone if only because it gives the landlord two parties against whom to take action. The tenant's adviser should seek to make the deletion suggested.

3.9.5 Conditions

The Landlord may impose any or all of the following conditions which are specified for the purposes of the Landlord and Tenant Act 1927 section 19(1A) on giving any consent for an assignment by the Tenant, and any such consent is to be treated as being subject to each of the following:

3.9.5.1 a condition that on or before any assignment and before giving occupation to the assignee, the Tenant requesting consent to assign, together with any former tenant who by virtue of the 1995 Act section 11 was not released on an earlier assignment of this Lease, must enter into an authorised guarantee agreement in favour of the Landlord in the terms set out in Schedule 8 THE AUTHORISED GUARANTEE AGREEMENT

3.9.5.2 a condition that if reasonably so required by the Landlord on an assignment to a limited company, the assignee must ensure that at least 2 directors of the company, or some other guarantor or guarantors acceptable to the Landlord, enter into direct covenants with the Landlord in the form of the guarantor's covenants contained in clause 6 GUARANTEE PROVISIONS with 'the Assignee' substituted for 'the Tenant'

3.9.5.3 a condition that upon or before any assignment, the Tenant making the request for consent to assign must <u>if applicable in the particular circumstances of the proposed assignment</u> give to the Landlord a copy of the health and safety file required to be maintained under the Construction (Design and Management) Regulations 1994 containing full details of all works undertaken to the Premises by that Tenant and

3.9.5.4 a condition that if, at any time before the assignment, the circumstances specified in clause 3.9.4, or any of them, apply, the Landlord may revoke the consent by written notice to the Tenant <u>with written reasons therefore</u>

3.9.6 Charging of the whole

The Tenant must not charge the whole of the Premises without the consent of the Landlord, whose consent may not be unreasonably withheld or delayed <u>PROVIDED ALWAYS that this clause is not to prevent the creation of a floating charge over all the assets of the Tenant for the purposes of his normal banking arrangements and the existence of any charge created by him for such purposes over acquired property at the date on which his interest in the Premises arose does not constitute a breach of this subclause</u>

3.9.7 Subletting

The Tenant must not sublet the whole <u>or part</u> of the Premises without the consent of the Landlord, whose consent may not be unreasonably withheld <u>or delayed</u>

3.9.5.3 The amendment is self-explanatory and seeks to make consideration by a landlord a wholly subjective one.

3.9.5.4 The proposed amendment seeks to give the tenant something against which to argue and reflects the landlord's obligation under the Landlord and Tenant Act 1988. If a tenant has detailed written reasons at least issue can be taken if the tenant or assignee disagrees.

3.9.6 Ideally the tenant should seek to delete this clause in its entirety but a landlord is unlikely to accept this. The primary reason for the deletion is that any financial institution taking a charge over the lease is most likely to have a greater covenant strength than that of the tenant and in theory, therefore, if that chargee enforced its security and took possession the landlord would be in a better position. However landlords are likely to be very suspicious about this and it's deletion is not likely to prove acceptable. The proviso which has been added seeks to ensure that the granting of debentures which affect the entirety of any corporate tenant's property portfolio is not prevented. It is unlikely, in the author's view, that a landlord would find this proviso unacceptable.

3.9.7 This amendment reflects and follows through the suggested amendment under clause 3.9.2.

3.9.8 Terms of a permitted sublease

Every permitted sublease must be granted, without a fine or premium, at a rent not less than ~~whichever is the greater of~~ the then open market rent payable in respect of the Premises to be approved by the Landlord before the sublease and to be determined by the Surveyor, acting as an expert and not as an arbitrator ~~and the Rent,~~ to be payable in advance on the days on which the Rent is payable under this Lease. Every permitted sublease must contain provisions approved by the Landlord:

3.9.8.1 for the upwards only review of the rent reserved by it, on the basis set out in Schedule 4 THE RENT AND RENT REVIEW and on the Review Dates

3.9.8.2 prohibiting the subtenant from doing or allowing anything in relation to the Premises inconsistent with or in breach of the provisions of this Lease

3.9.8.3 for re-entry by the sublandlord on breach of any covenant by the subtenant

3.9.8.4 imposing an absolute prohibition against all dealings with the Premises other than assignment or subletting of the whole or subletting of a Permitted Part

3.9.8.5 prohibiting assignment or subletting of the whole or subletting of a Permitted Part of the Premises without the prior consent of the Landlord under this Lease

3.9.8.6 requiring the assignee on any assignment of the sublease to enter into direct covenants with the Landlord to the same effect as those contained in clause 3.9.9 SUBTENANT'S DIRECT COVENANTS

3.9.8.7 requiring on each assignment of the sublease that the assignor enters into an authorised guarantee agreement in favour of the Landlord in the terms set out in Schedule 8 THE AUTHORISED GUARANTEE AGREEMENT but adapted to suit the circumstances in which the guarantee is given

3.9.8.8 prohibiting the subtenant from holding on trust for another or permitting another to share or occupy the whole or any part of the Premises

3.9.8.9 imposing in relation to any permitted assignment or subletting the same obligations for registration with the Landlord as are contained in this Lease in relation to dispositions by the Tenant

3.9.8.10 imposing in relation to any permitted subletting the same obligations as are contained in this clause 3.9.8 and in clauses 3.9.9 SUBTENANT'S DIRECT COVENANTS, 3.9.10 ENFORCEMENT ETC OF SUBLEASES and 3.9.11 SUBLEASE RENT REVIEW and

3.9.8 In recent recessionary times with falling rents it was often impossible for tenants to sublet either a part or the whole of the premises because of the existence of a clause such as the one originally drafted here. If rents have fallen and the open market rent is in fact less than the passing rent it is going to be difficult, if not impossible for a tenant to find a subtenant prepared to pay the passing rent. No properly advised prospective subtenant would accept this. It is, therefore, only fair that a tenant should have the ability to sublet at what is an open market rent in order to subsidise his over-rented premises. Landlords are in practice not likely to be in a worse position and any concerns of the landlord can be met if any such sublease is '*contracted out*'. Landlords still have the benefit of the original tenant covenant (and possibly a guarantor) and can insist on an open market rent review in the sublease. Any concern a landlord expresses that he may be stuck with a lower passing rent should he forfeit the head lease is unfounded. If the head lease is forfeited, a subtenant can apply for relief against forfeiture (by virtue of an application for a vesting order) but relief from forfeiture is most likely to be granted to a subtenant at a rental equivalent to the old head lease rent (apportioned if the sublease applies to only part of the premises comprised in the old head lease) although the courts do retain a discretion to fix a 'fair rent' (*London Bridge Buildings Co v Thomson* (1903) 89 LT 50).

3.9.8.4 This ties in with the amendment introduced into the definitions section under clause 1.30 (new) which defined a *Permitted Part* in relation to which a sublease can be granted.

~~3.9.8.11 excluding the provisions of sections 24–28 of the 1954 Act from the letting created by the sublease~~

3.9.9 Subtenant's direct covenants

Before any permitted subletting, the Tenant must ensure that the subtenant enters into a direct covenant with the Landlord that while the subtenant is bound by the tenant covenants of the sublease and while he is bound by an authorised guarantee agreement the subtenant will observe and perform the tenant covenants contained in this Lease except the covenant to pay the rent reserved by this Lease and in that sublease.

~~3.9.10 Requirement for an exclusion order~~

~~The Tenant must not grant a sublease or permit a subtenant to occupy the Premises unless an order has been obtained under section 38(4) of the 1954 Act.~~

3.9.10 Enforcement, waiver and variation of subleases

The Tenant must enforce the performance and observance by the subtenant of the provisions of every permitted sublease, and must not at any time either expressly or by implication <u>knowingly</u> waive any breach of the covenants or conditions on the part of any subtenant or assignee of any sublease, or (without the consent of the Landlord <u>whose consent is not to be unreasonably withheld or delayed</u>) vary the terms or accept a surrender of any permitted sublease.

3.9.11 Sublease rent review

In relation to any permitted sublease:

3.9.11.1 the Tenant must ensure that the rent is reviewed in accordance with the terms of the sublease

3.9.11.2 the Tenant must not agree the reviewed rent with the subtenant without the approval of the Landlord <u>such approval not to be unreasonably withheld or delayed</u>

3.9.11.3 where the sublease provides such an option, the Tenant must not, without the approval of the Landlord <u>such approval not to be unreasonably withheld or delayed,</u> agree whether the third party determining the revised rent in default of agreement should act as an arbitrator or as an expert

3.9.11.4 the Tenant must not, without the approval of the Landlord <u>such approval not to be unreasonably withheld or delayed</u>, agree any appointment of a person to act as the third party determining the revised rent

3.9.8.11 For management reasons the landlord may wish to ensure that any subtenants do not obtain security of tenure. It will in practice be a question of the bargaining strength of the parties as to whose view will prevail. The author has deleted the subclause on the basis that it is up to the landlord to come up with compelling reasons as to why security of tenure should be excluded from the proposed subletting. If the landlord has the contractual right to refuse a proposed subtenant on the basis of covenant strength, there is a question mark over any argument he puts forward arguing against security of tenure for a covenant which by agreeing to the subletting in the first place satisfies its own tests (see clause 3.5.8).

3.9.10 (delete) This is simply a belt and braces provision for the landlord in relation to the *contracting out* of any sublease. As mentioned above in relation to clause 3.9.8.11 it is a question of the relative bargaining strength of the parties as to whose arguments will win the day. In theory at least the requirement that any subtenancy be subject to an exclusion order may make subletting that bit more difficult for the tenant in an already difficult market place.

3.9.10 (new) The amendments here are self-explanatory (see clauses 3.5.4 and 3.7.2.2). The tenant, as the subtenant's landlord, cannot be expected to police the premises every single day and is only likely to become aware of a breach by the subtenant when something goes wrong. Hence the addition of the word '*knowingly*'. The second amendment imposes an obligation on the landlord to act reasonably and no such statutory implication exists in these circumstances.

3.9.11.2 This amendment provides that when deciding whether or not to agree to the reviewed rent with the subtenant, the head landlord is under a contractual obligation to behave reasonably. Again no such statutory obligation exists in such circumstances and such a requirement must be spelt out.

3.9.11.3 See the comments under clause 3.9.11.2. above.

3.9.11.4 See the comments under clause 3.9.11.2.above.

3.9.11.5 the Tenant must incorporate as part of his representations to that third party representations reasonably required by the Landlord and

3.9.11.6 the Tenant must give notice to the Landlord of the details of the determination of every rent review within 28 days

3.9.12 Registration of permitted dealings

Within 28 days of any assignment, sublease, or subunderlease, or any transmission or other devolution relating to the Premises, the Tenant must produce a certified copy of any relevant document for registration with the Landlord's solicitor, and must pay the Landlord's solicitor's charges for registration of ~~at least~~ £25.00 plus value added tax

3.9.13 Sharing with a Group Company

Notwithstanding clause 3.9.1 ALIENATION PROHIBITED, the Tenant may share the occupation of the whole or any part of the Premises with a Group Company

3.10 Nuisance and residential restrictions

3.10.1 Nuisance

The Tenant must not do anything on the Premises or allow anything to remain on them that may be or become or cause a legal nuisance, ~~or annoyance, disturbance, inconvenience,~~ injury or damage to the Landlord or his tenants or the owners or occupiers of adjacent or neighbouring premises PROVIDED ALWAYS that the proper use of the Premises as offices by the Tenant shall not in any circumstances constitute a breach of this obligation

3.10.2 Auctions, trades and immoral purposes

The Tenant must not use the Premises for a sale by auction or for any dangerous, noxious, noisy or offensive trade, business, manufacture or occupation, or any illegal or immoral act or purpose PROVIDED ALWAYS that the proper use of the Premises as offices by the Tenant shall not in any circumstances constitute a breach of this obligation

3.9.11.5 See the comments under clause 3.9.11.2. above.

3.9.12 The amendment here is designed to give certainty. Like everything else within the confines of a commercial lease, many landlords are increasingly seeking to impose the cost of any involvement they have in the management of the premises on the tenant and the tenant will often consider such charges to be unreasonable. Deletion of the words '*at least*' gives a fixed fee liability and prevents the tenant from being at the mercy of his landlord.

3.9.13 (new) Any corporate tenant that is a member (or indeed likely to become a member) of a wider group should insist upon a provision being incorporated in a lease which gives maximum flexibility in terms of occupation with other group companies. A landlord would normally find such a group sharing clause acceptable but may add a further proviso to the effect that such sharing would be acceptable only for so long as the two companies remain members of the same group (see clause 1.11) *and* in so far as the sharing of occupation does not give rise to a new tenancy between those two companies. This is an acceptable compromise in the author's view. It may also be worth trying to amend the group sharing clause shown to include any franchises or concessionaires who may wish to share occupation on similar terms to that of a group company.

3.10.1 As originally drafted this clause is vague, incapable of legal certainty and very subjective. What is one man's annoyance is another man's pleasure. Annoyance, disturbance and inconvenience have no foundation in law as they are not recognised torts. The amendment seeks to ensure that what can and cannot be done by the tenant is set against some proper legal barometer. The proviso added at the end is self-explanatory but is an important addition to give the tenant peace of mind in using the premises for the permitted use set out in paragraph 1.1 of Schedule 5. The landlord will have taken into account the tenant's proposed use of the premises at the time it decided either to grant the lease or consent to the assignment and this should be sufficient to ensure that the tenant's proper use of the offices does not constitute a breach of this clause.

3.10.2 The author has added a similar proviso at the end of this clause for the same reason as that stated at clause 3.10.1. For many years the author tried to ascertain why the antiquated notion of banning auctions existed. Finding little to help in texts he was grateful to a practitioner who explained that landlords were simply concerned that a '... a mass of people stampeding at an auction was likely to damage the fabric of the premises, something a landlord wanted to avoid!' Readers will draw their own conclusion as to whether references to auctions should remain!

3.10.3 Residential use, sleeping and animals

The Tenant must not use the Premises as sleeping accommodation or for residential purposes, or keep any animal on them

3.11 Costs of applications, notices and recovery of arrears

The Tenant must pay to the Landlord ~~on an indemnity basis~~ all reasonable and proper costs, fees, charges, disbursements and expenses (including without prejudice to the generality of the above those payable to counsel, solicitors, surveyors and bailiffs) incurred by the Landlord in relation to or incidental to:

3.11.1 every application made by the Tenant for a consent or licence required by the provisions of this Lease~~, whether it is granted, refused or offered subject to any qualification or condition, or the application is withdrawn~~ unless the same is unlawfully or unreasonably withheld or delayed or offered subject to some unlawful or unreasonable condition

3.11.2 the lawful and proper [contemplation], preparation and service of a notice under the Law of Property Act 1925 section 146, or the lawful and proper contemplation or taking of proceedings under sections 146 or 147 of that Act, even if forfeiture is avoided otherwise than by relief granted by the court

3.11.3 the recovery or attempted recovery of arrears of rent or other sums due under this Lease and

3.11.4 any lawful and proper steps taken in direct connection with the preparation and service of a schedule of dilapidations during or within six months after the end of the Term

3.11 The addition of the words *reasonable and proper* shown in the text in substitution for the deleted words is, in the author's view, still sufficient protection for the landlord. If the landlord has incurred unreasonable or improper charges then there is no reason why, on the indemnity basis originally sought, a tenant should be liable for these and hence the deletion.

3.11.1 If the landlord behaves unlawfully or unreasonably in withholding or delaying consent or offers the consent subject to unlawful or unreasonable conditions or qualifications, there is no reason why a tenant should be responsible for reimbursing the costs that the landlord has incurred in coming to this unsustainable conclusion. All that the tenant is asking the landlord to do is to conduct himself in a manner consistent with both his statutory and contractual obligations. If the landlord's behaviour is inconsistent with these obligations then he must take account of the possible cost implications and also appreciate that the tenant may pursue a claim against him for damages under the Landlord and Tenant Act 1988.

3.11.2 The amendment here ensures that what the landlord *contemplates* is undertaken in a lawful and proper manner. The author's natural instinct is actually to delete the word 'contemplate' because it is almost impossible to know with any degree of certainty what 'proper contemplation' is. If 'contemplation' becomes reality then the landlord will actually set these grounds out in any notice he serves. Therefore this word adds nothing.

3.11.4 The first amendment ensures that the landlord does not recover costs in a dilapidations claim for anything other than those incurred and for its proper purposes. The amendment at the end of the clause is designed to ensure that the tenant's liability for costs in respect of any such claim is limited to a reasonable time after the end of the lease term. There can be few things more uncertain for a tenant than not knowing whether or not a schedule of dilapidation is coming. The longer the time lapse between the end of the term (or the date when the tenant vacates) and the date when the schedule is prepared and served on the tenant the more and more difficult it is to prove (from a landlord's point of view) that the disrepair is a result of the tenant's failure to comply with its repairing obligations rather than simply wear and tear by the passage of time. By imposing a contractual timescale, there is, at least, a cut-off point without having to rely on the statutory limitation periods in relation to the costs liability.

3.12 Planning and development

3.12.1 Compliance with the Planning Acts

The Tenant must observe and comply with the provisions and requirements of the Planning Acts affecting the Premises and their use~~, and must indemnify the Landlord, and keep him indemnified, both during and following the end of the Term, against all losses in respect of any contravention of those Acts~~

3.12.2 Consent for applications

The Tenant must not make any application for planning permission without the consent of the Landlord such consent not to be unreasonably withheld or delayed

3.12.3 Permissions and notices

The Tenant must obtain any planning permissions and serve any notices that may be required to carry out any development on or at the Premises

3.12.4 Charges and levies

Subject only to any statutory direction to the contrary, the Tenant must pay and satisfy any charge or levy that may subsequently be imposed under the Planning Acts in respect of carrying out or maintaining any development on or at the Premises

3.12.5 Pre-conditions for development

Notwithstanding any consent that may be granted by the Landlord under this Lease, the Tenant must not carry out any development on or at the Premises until all necessary notices under the Planning Acts have been served and copies produced to the Landlord, all necessary permissions under the Planning Acts have been obtained and produced to the Landlord, and the Landlord (acting reasonably) has acknowledged that every necessary planning permission is acceptable to him (such acknowledgement not to be unreasonably withheld or delayed). The Landlord may refuse to acknowledge his acceptance of a planning permission on the grounds that any condition contained in it or anything omitted from it or the period referred to in it would in the reasonable opinion of the Surveyor be, or be likely to be, prejudicial to the Landlord or to his reversionary interest in the Premises, the Building or any of his adjoining property whether during or following the end of the Term

3.12.6 Completion of development

Where a condition of any planning permission granted for development begun before the end of the Term requires works to be carried out to the Premises by a date after the end of the Term, the Tenant must, unless the Landlord directs otherwise, finish those works before the end of the Term

3.12.1 Landlords' advisers often prepare an initial draft lease which is often very heavily biased in favour of landlords. The need for indemnities anywhere in the lease should therefore be questioned by the tenant. As well as having all the tortious, contractual and self-help remedies available to a landlord to then seek an indemnity is, in the author's view, unfair to the tenant. Hence *all* references to indemnities from tenant to landlord in the lease have been deleted. It is, quite clearly, a question of the relative bargaining positions of the parties as to whether or not this is likely to be acceptable. The tenant should argue long and hard to ensure that his arguments win the day.

3.12.2 The amendment prevents the tenant being held to ransom by the landlord and avoids a situation arising when the landlord is obliged to consent to an alteration or improvement but then does not give consent to the necessary planning application.

3.12.5 While likely to be a very emotive issue for the landlord (on the grounds that any *development* which takes place may raise the possibility of a diminution in the value of his interest in the premises) the amendments are intended to ensure that in all the circumstances the landlord acts reasonably. An absolute prohibition with the consequent ability of a landlord to frustrate fair and reasonable requests from the tenant is likely, in reality, only to lead to one of two things: either an abuse of the landlord's dominant position or some form of ransom payment being required.

3.12.7 Security for compliance with conditions

In any case where a planning permission is granted subject to conditions, and if the Landlord reasonably so requires, the Tenant must provide sufficient security for his compliance with the conditions ~~and must not implement the planning permission until the security has been provided~~

3.12.8 Appeal against refusal or conditions

If reasonably required by the Landlord to do so, ~~but~~ and at ~~his own~~ the Landlord's cost, the Tenant must appeal against any refusal of planning permission or the imposition of any conditions on a planning permission relating to the Premises following an application for planning permission by the Tenant.

3.13 Plans, documents and information

3.13.1 Evidence of compliance with this Lease

If so requested (but not more than once in any calendar year), the Tenant must produce to the Landlord or the Surveyor any plans, documents and other evidence the Landlord reasonably requires to satisfy himself that the provisions of this Lease have been complied with

3.13.2 Information for renewal or rent review

~~3.13.2.1 If so requested, the Tenant must produce to the Landlord, the Surveyor or any person acting as the third party determining the Rent in default of agreement between the Landlord and the Tenant under the provisions for rent review contained in this Lease, any information requested in writing in relation to any pending or intended step under the 1954 Act or the implementation of any provisions for rent review~~

3.13.2.1 if so requested, the Tenant must, within one month of the change taking place, notify the Landlord of any changes in his VAT status

~~**3.14 Indemnities**~~

~~The Tenant must keep the Landlord fully indemnified against all losses arising directly or indirectly out of any act, omission or negligence of the Tenant, or any persons at the Premises expressly or impliedly with his authority or any breach or non-observance by the Tenant of the covenants, conditions or other provisions of this Lease or any of the matters to which this demise is subject~~

3.12.7 The same points apply here as those stated above in relation to clauses 3.12.2 and 3.12.5.

3.12.8 If the failure to obtain planning consent following a tenant's application is likely to be detrimental to the landlord's interest, he may request that the tenant appeals against any planning refusal. If this is a decision made by the landlord then there is absolutely no reason why the landlord should not pay for it. If such an appeal is not likely to affect the tenant's ability to continue to use the premises for its permitted use (so that the tenant does not wish to appeal) then it would seem unreasonable for the landlord to request that such an appeal be made. The amendments seek to cater for both these concerns.

3.13.1 The author's natural inclination would be to delete this clause in its entirety. A landlord will have reserved powers to himself (eg rights of access to inspect) to satisfy himself that the tenant is complying with his obligation. This clause, unfairly, puts the onus on the tenant to prove that he is not in breach! The proposed amendments ensure that the landlord does not use this clause for nuisance value.

3.13.2 If landlord and tenant have been unable to agree the new level of rent, despite having tried to do so, then the provision is wholly unacceptable. Rent review negotiations and lease renewal negotiations are likely to be two occasions when there may be potential litigation between the parties. The tenant should not accept a provision whereby it is obliged to show its hand before being advised to do so by its professional advisers and clauses such as this should be strongly resisted if only for this reason.

3.14 (deleted) As was previously alluded to under clause 3.12.1 in consequence of all the tortious, contractual, self-help and other remedies available to a landlord, a general indemnity is far too wide ranging to be readily acceptable to a tenant. Common law and statute adequately deals with the losses an aggrieved party can recover and an indemnity such as this goes beyond the general remoteness of damage test. It is the author's view that, as a matter of policy, indemnities should be resisted but, clearly, the outcome of this particular debate is going to be decided ultimately by the relative bargaining strengths of the parties. Institutional landlords certainly have their own views! Tenants and their advisers must nevertheless appreciate fully the consequences of agreeing to such a clause.

3.14 Reletting boards and viewing

Where the Tenant has no right or no longer has the right to a new lease of the Premises pursuant to the relevant provisions of the 1954 Act Tthe Tenant must permit the Landlord to enter the Premises at any reasonable time (on reasonable prior written notice) during the last 6 months of the Contractual Term and at any time thereafter and whenever the Lease Rents or any part of them are in arrear and unpaid (and not disputed) for longer than 14 21 days and to fix and retain anywhere on the Premises a board advertising them for reletting. While any such board is on the Premises to which the Tenant has not objected the Tenant must permit viewing of them at reasonable times of the day

3.15 Obstruction and encroachment

3.15.1 Obstruction of windows

The Tenant must not knowingly stop up, darken or obstruct any window or light belonging to the Premises

3.15.2 Encroachments

The Tenant must at the Landlord's sole cost and expense take all reasonable steps to prevent the construction of any new window, light, opening, doorway, path, passage, pipe or the making of any encroachment or the acquisition of any easement in relation to the Premises and must notify the Landlord as soon as reasonably practicable after becoming aware of the same immediately if any such thing is constructed, encroachment is made or easement acquired, or if any attempt is made to encroach or acquire an easement. At the reasonable request and cost of the Landlord the Tenant must adopt such reasonable means as are required to prevent the making of any encroachment or the acquisition of any easement PROVIDED ALWAYS that the Tenant shall not be obliged by virtue of this subclause or any other provision contained in this Lease be obliged to take any steps likely to interfere with its beneficial use and occupation of the Premises

3.16 Yielding up

At the end of the Term the Tenant must yield up the Premises with vacant possession, decorated and repaired in accordance with and in the condition required by the provisions of this Lease, give up all keys of the Premises to the Landlord, remove tenant's fixtures and fittings if requested to do so by the Landlord and remove all signs erected by the Tenant or any of his predecessors in title in, on or near the Premises, immediately making good as soon as reasonably practicable any physical damage caused to the Premises by their removal

3.14 (new) If the tenant is likely to want to remain in the premises at the end of the term then, clearly, there is no need for the landlord to be looking to re-let and many of the proposed amendments are likely to be unnecessary. However, it would be rare for a tenant to know its future intentions when the lease is being negotiated! Where, however, a tenant does not wish to remain in occupation the amendments seek to ensure that any viewing etc is undertaken so as to cause minimum disruption to the tenant's occupation.

3.15.1 The amendment here introduces the element of knowledge on the part of the tenant.

3.15.2 The matters with which this clause purports to deal with are ones which the landlord may, reasonably or otherwise, consider adversely affect the value of his reversionary interest. The amendments will prevent the tenant being out of pocket in seeking to maintain the status quo (and value!) of the landlord's reversion and ensure that any such works which are required are undertaken at the cost of the landlord and that they do not interfere with the tenant's occupation or use of the property.

3.16 It is absolutely fair that the landlord should have the property back at the end of the term decorated and repaired in accordance with the tenant's obligations set out in the lease. What is potentially contentious is whether or not fixtures and fittings which the tenant may be prepared to leave (and which may actually enhance the value or marketability of the premises) should be removed by the tenant, if indeed their ownership has not already passed to the landlord. The amendments seek to introduce the concept of reasonableness into this particular debate (and not leave it to be decided by the landlord from his own totally subjective viewpoint). The amendments towards the end of the clause seek to ensure that any liability in consequence of such removal by the tenant is limited to physical damage caused to the premises and does not extend to any form of pecuniary loss a landlord may claim.

3.17 Interest on arrears

The Tenant must pay interest on any of the Lease Rents or other sums due under this Lease that are not paid within [21] days of ~~on~~ the date due, whether formally demanded or not, the interest to be recoverable as rent~~. Nothing in this clause is to entitle the Tenant to withhold or delay any payment of the Rent or any other sum due under this Lease or affect the rights of the Landlord in relation to any non-payment~~

3.18 Statutory notices

The Tenant must give the Landlord full particulars of any notice, direction, order or proposal relating to the Premises made, given or issued to the Tenant by any government department or local, public, regulatory or other authority or court as soon as reasonably practicable following ~~within 2 days of~~ receipt, and if so reasonably requested by the Landlord must produce it to the Landlord. The Tenant must as soon as reasonably practicable ~~without delay~~ take all ~~necessary~~ reasonable steps to comply with the notice, direction or order. At the request and cost of the Landlord, ~~but at his own cost,~~ the Tenant must make or join with the Landlord in making any objection or representation the Landlord deems expedient against or in respect of a notice, direction, order or proposal PROVIDED ALWAYS the Tenant shall not by virtue of the provisions of this subclause or any other provision contained in this Lease be obliged to take or join in any such steps likely to affect its beneficial enjoyment or use of the Premises in accordance with the provisions of this Lease

3.19 Keyholders

The Tenant must ensure that at all times the Landlord has ~~[and the local police force have]~~ written notice of the name, home address and home telephone number of one ~~at least 2~~ keyholder~~s~~ of the Premises

3.20 Viewing on sale of reversion

The Tenant must at any reasonable time during the Term and on reasonable prior written notice , permit prospective purchasers of the Landlord's reversion or any other interest superior to the Term, or agents instructed in connection with the sale of the reversion or such an interest, to view the Premises without interruption provided they have the prior written authority of the Landlord or his agents

3.21 Defective premises

As soon as reasonably practicable after becoming aware of the same ~~T~~the Tenant must give notice to the Landlord of any defect in the

3.17 Periods of grace are now fairly commonplace in commercial leases and this clause seeks to enshrine, contractually, a period of grace when payment of rent and other sums fall due. If a period of grace is accepted then, clearly, the second sentence in this clause can be deleted. Even if a period of grace is not acceptable to a landlord, a tenant should still seek to delete the second sentence to ensure that the clause does not conflict with any lease provisions dealing with set off (see clause 2.1.1).

3.18 The amendments to the first two sentences will seek to ensure that there is no breach in failing to notify the landlord within the time period stated. There may be a multitude of reasons why it is not possible to comply with the strict timetable set out and the amendment caters for these eventualities. The amendment dealing with the cost of compliance ensures that, particularly in relation to short-term lettings, the tenant is not out of pocket. The fairness of such a provision would have to be judged in the overall context of the transaction. The proviso seeks to ensure that the tenant is not obliged to take any steps likely to affect its occupation and use of the property.

3.19 There may be circumstances where it is totally inappropriate to have this clause in a lease of office premises in any event whether the police need to be involved will vary from letting to letting. However, it is likely to be in the tenant's interest as much as the landlord that this information is available, eg in the case of burglary. It may be however that, depending on the circumstances of the particular letting, it is not possible to give details of *two* key holders and one may have to suffice.

3.20 The amendments to this clause give the tenant an element of control over when people view the premises with the potential for disruption and rumours this may cause (see clause 3.8.1).

3.21 It is unlikely that as soon as a defect manifests itself in the premises the tenant will be aware of it (unless there is something patently obvious) and even more unlikely that the tenant (or at least the employees within the premises) will be aware that the existence of such a defect imposes

Premises that might give rise to an obligation on the Landlord to do or refrain from doing anything in order to comply with the provisions of this Lease or the duty of care imposed on the Landlord, whether pursuant to the Defective Premises Act 1972 or otherwise, and must at all times display and maintain any reasonable notices the Landlord from time to time reasonably requires him to display at the Premises

3.22 Replacement guarantor

3.22.1 Guarantor replacement events

In this clause 3.23 references to a 'guarantor replacement event' are references, in the case of an individual, to death, bankruptcy, having a receiving order made against him or having a receiver appointed under the Mental Health Act 1983, and, in the case of a company, to passing a resolution to wind up, entering into liquidation or having a receiver appointed

3.22.2 Action on occurrence of a guarantor replacement event

Where during the relevant Liability Period a guarantor replacement event occurs to the Guarantor or any person who has entered into an authorised guarantee agreement, the Tenant must as soon as reasonably practicable after becoming aware of the same give notice of the event to the Landlord ~~within 14 days of his becoming aware of it~~. If so reasonably required by the Landlord, the Tenant must within 28 days use all reasonable endeavours to obtain some other person or corporate body acceptable to the Landlord to execute a guarantee in the form of the Guarantor's covenants in clause 6 GUARANTEE PROVISIONS or the authorised guarantee agreement in Schedule 8 THE AUTHORISED GUARANTEE AGREEMENT, as the case may be, for the residue of the relevant Liability Period and upon the execution of such an alternative guarantee the original guarantor or person who has entered into the authorised guarantee agreement and/or their estates shall be unconditionally released from all past present or future liability

3.23 Exercise of the Landlord's rights

Subject to the provisions of clause 4.4 ~~T~~the Tenant must permit the Landlord to exercise any of the rights granted to him by virtue of the provisions of this Lease at all times during the Term without interruption or interference

3.24 The Office Covenants

The Tenant must observe and perform the Office Covenants

a statutory duty on the landlord! The amendments to this clause aim to deal with these concerns from a tenant's point of view and strike a fair balance between the obligations on the part of the tenant and the statutory duties on the part of the landlord.

3.22.2 Ideally this clause should be ditched in its entirety. It may be extremely difficult for a tenant to find a substitute guarantor. In the event that it is possible it is vital to ensure a formal release is obtained from the original guarantor. The first amendment to this clause is self-explanatory. Bearing in mind the nature of *guarantor replacement events* it will not always be possible for the tenant to be aware of such matters. A short fixed timetable is therefore unacceptable. The second amendment meets the situation where the status of the tenant has changed during the time the guarantee has subsisted so that it would, by an objective standard, no longer be reasonable to request a guarantor. The final amendment ensures, for the avoidance of doubt, that there is no duplication from the tenant's point of view and no dispute as to whether or not the original guarantor or any party who has entered into the authorised guarantee agreement is still potentially liable as the amendment expressly provides for his release.

3.23 The amendment provides that any access rights exercised by the landlord are exercised in accordance with a landlord's covenant contained in new clause 4.4.

3.25 The Services

The Tenant must observe and perform his obligations contained in Schedule 6 THE SERVICE CHARGE AND SERVICES

~~3.27 Costs of grant of this lease~~

~~The Tenant must pay the fees and disbursements of the Landlord's solicitors, agents and surveyors and all other costs and expenses incurred by the Landlord in relation to the negotiation, preparation, execution and grant of this lease and the stamp duty on the counterpart~~

~~3.28 Consent to the Landlord's release~~

~~The Tenant must not unreasonably withhold consent to a request made by the Landlord under the 1995 Act section 8 for a release from all or any of the landlord covenants of this Lease~~

4 THE LANDLORD'S COVENANTS

The Landlord covenants with the Tenant to observe and perform the requirements of this clause 4

4.1 Quiet enjoyment

The Landlord covenants with the Tenant to permit the Tenant peaceably and quietly to hold and enjoy the Premises without any interruption or disturbance from or by the Landlord or any person claiming under or in trust for him or by title paramount

3.27 It is to be hoped that in today's climate that the old practice of tenants having to be responsible for landlord's costs has now, to a large extent, fallen by the wayside. Tenants have their own legal fees to pay and there can be, in the author's view, no sustainable reason why on the grant of a lease the tenant should pick up both his own legal (and other) costs and those of the landlord. Indeed the Costs of Leases Act 1958 states that each party should pay their own costs (in the absence of agreement).

Landlords will often argue that it is a historical convention but during recessionary times the author certainly has acted on a number of occasions for tenants when landlords actually agreed to pay the tenant's fees! Should tenants therefore be arguing for a shifting convention? As the property market follows its normal cyclical path of undersupply/overdemand and vice versa with the consequential shift in relative bargaining of landlords and tenants, tenants can in the appropriate marketplace insist that each party is responsible for its own costs!

3.28 This is quite a useful (and clever) clause from a landlord's point of view if he can get away with it!. However, in the author's view, there are going to be few occasions where such a clause should be agreed to by the tenant right at the outset of the lease. In the same way that any application for licence to assign by the tenant will be rigorously scrutinised on its merits at the appropriate time by the landlord, the question of consent to the landlord's release (should it dispose of its reversion) should likewise be subject to the same scrutiny at the appropriate time. In addition it should be noted that statements which attempt to limit the landlord's liability are unlikely to withstand the anti-avoidance provisions contained in section 25 of the Landlord and Tenant (Covenants) Act 1995 and such a covenant by the tenant to release a landlord automatically is unlikely to fall within the exceptions contained in section 26 of that Act. A landlord should be content in the knowledge that if a tenant unreasonably objects to the landlord being released when he sells the reversion he does have a statutory right to apply for a release.

THE LANDLORD'S COVENANTS

4.1 This amendment, while often missed by tenants and not readily accepted by landlords, is really quite vital from a tenant's point of view. Without reference to *title paramount*, the landlord is only liable for the acts of persons in so far as they are his successors in title or have authority from him to do the acts of which the tenant is complaining. So if a subtenant holds premises under a lease containing a limited quiet enjoyment covenant on the part of his landlord (eg a clause where there is no reference to title paramount) only for the subtenant to be evicted by the head landlord because the head rent has not been paid, this does *not* constitute a breach of the covenant for quiet enjoyment by the tenant's landlord and no claim for damages can be made against him. The words must be included.

4.2 The Services

4.2.1 Provision of the Services

~~If the Tenant pays the service charge and observes his obligations under this Lease,~~ Tthe Landlord must use his best ~~reasonable~~ endeavours to provide the Services

4.2.2 Relief from liability

The Landlord is not to be liable to the Tenant for any breach of his obligations under clause 4.2.1, where the breach is caused by something beyond his control (provided he uses reasonable endeavours to remedy the breach) except to the extent that the breach:

4.2.2.1 could have been prevented or

4.2.2.2 its consequences could have been lessened or

4.2.2.3 the time during which its consequences were experienced could have been shortened by the exercise of reasonable skill by the Landlord or those undertaking the obligation on his behalf

4.2.3 Variation and withholding of the Services

The Landlord may add to, withhold or vary the Services if (acting reasonably) he considers the addition, withholding or variation to be necessary or desirable in the interests of good estate arrangement or for the comfort and convenience of the tenants or occupiers in the Building even if it increases the Landlord's Expenses (provided the Tenant's beneficial use and enjoyment of the Premises is not impaired or interfered with) or if he is required to do so by a competent authority

4.2.4 Special services

Any services rendered to the Tenant by staff employed by the Landlord, other than services referred to in paragraph 6-3, are to be deemed to be special services for which, and for the consequences of which, the Tenant will be entirely responsible. The Tenant is not to be entitled to any services from such staff that may in any way whatever interfere with the performance of their duties to the Landlord

4.3 Similar Leases

The Landlord covenants with the Tenant not to allow any other party to occupy all or any parts of the Building other than pursuant to a lease in materially the same form as this Lease

4.2.1 The first part of the amendment deletes the precondition requirement for provision of the services. In reality it will be virtually impossible for a landlord to police and operate such a precondition, especially in the case of a multi-let building. If one tenant defaults on a precondition is the landlord going to cut off provision of the services to all the occupiers? This is obviously most unlikely and, therefore, the precondition is in many instances a nonsense and does not provide any realistic sanction against the tenant. An additional reason for its deletion would be to ensure that if a tenant, for example, was in arrears on the service charge payments (eg because of a dispute) he would still be able to bring an action against the landlord for non-performance of the services and would not be barred out. The second amendment seeks to impose on the landlord the highest possible duty to provide what will no doubt be vitally important services required by the tenant (see clause 5.6.3.1).

4.2.2 Ideally the tenant would wish to delete this clause in its entirety and argue that an exclusion clause would need to comply with the provisions of section 2 of the Unfair Contract Terms Act 1977. However, the question of whether or not that particular piece of legislation applies to service charge provisions contained in a lease is unresolved and has been the subject of much academic debate. If the exclusion clause is caught by the Unfair Contract Terms Act 1977 then the qualified covenant approach adopted here, which seeks to limit the circumstances in which the landlord will be in breach, may indeed satisfy the requirements of section 2 of the Act.

4.2.3 The first amendment to this clause brings an element of objectivity to determining what additional services may be in the interests of the tenant (and other tenants in the same building). The second amendment seeks to reinforce this. The proviso prohibits any variation or change to the services which would or might result in the tenant being left in a situation which is detrimental to his occupation and use.

4.3 (new) This additional covenant imposes on the landlord an obligation to grant leases to other tenants in the building on terms materially the same to ensure that there is an element of management consistency and this, coupled with the provisions contained in clause 4.5(new) below, gives the tenant the comfort of knowing that other parties occupy the building on broadly similar terms and will, for example, be making service charge payments. This will help reassure the tenant that nothing is likely to occur in other parts of the building which is likely to be detrimental to his own occupation.

4.4 Exercising Rights

In exercising the rights reserved to the Landlord by this Lease which involve entry on to the Premises the Landlord must:

4.4.1 cause and ensure that those exercising such rights on its behalf cause as little damage as is possible to the Premises and as little disturbance and inconvenience as possible to the Landlord and occupier

4.4.2 make good (at its own sole cost and expense) any damage caused in the exercise of such right and

4.4.3 indemnify the Tenant and any other occupiers of the Premises and keep them indemnified against all damage and loss suffered by them arising directly or indirectly out of the exercise of such right

4.5 Enforcing Covenants

The Landlord covenants to enforce the covenants on the part of the tenants contained in other leases in the Building

4.6 Environmental Matters

The Landlord covenants that it will as soon as reasonably practicable and at its own sole cost and expense undertake any works in relation to the Building required to comply with any environmental regulation, condition or legislation PROVIDED ALWAYS that no such cost or expense should be recharged to the tenants in the Building via the service charge or otherwise

5 INSURANCE

5.1 Warranty as to convictions

The Tenant warrants that before the execution of this document he has disclosed to the Landlord in writing any conviction, judgment or finding of any court or tribunal of which it is aware relating to the Tenant or any director, other officer or major shareholder of the Tenant of such a nature as to be likely to affect the decision of any insurer or underwriter to grant or to continue insurance of any of the Insured Risks

5.2 Covenant to insure

The Landlord covenants with the Tenant to insure the Building,[in the joint names of the Landlord and the Tenant] ~~if the Tenant pays the Insurance Rent,~~ unless the insurance is vitiated by any act of the Tenant or by anyone at the Building expressly or by implication with his authority and under his control

4.4 (new) This clause is self-explanatory. Landlords may well baulk at such a provision, but the author's view is that it is perfectly fair and reasonable although for the reasons given at clause 3.14 (deleted) the landlord could legitimately resist the indemnity referred to in clause 4.4.3.

4.5 (new) This new clause, coupled with clause 4.3(new) above, protects the position of the tenant by ensuring that nothing untoward is done by any other tenant in the building which is likely to detrimentally affect the complaining tenant's own use and occupation. The traditional view was that the covenant for quiet enjoyment granted by the landlord was *not* sufficient either to enable one tenant to bring an action against his landlord for his failure to ensure that another tenant complied with his contractual obligations contained in his own lease or to bring an action directly against the defaulting tenant. Tenants may now be able to rely on the recent decision in *Chartered Trust plc v Davies* [1997] 2 EGLR 83, CA, where it was held that there was a duty on the landlord in certain circumstances to ensure that one tenant's use of premises did not materially interfere with the use and enjoyment of other premises by a neighbouring tenant. However, it is much better to try and deal with the matter specifically and this clause attempts to do this. A compromise, if a landlord resists is to agree to inclusion of the clause, '... *at the cost of the tenant* ...'.

4.6 The landlord will either have satisfied himself about the environmental status of the site or the building prior to its construction (a site survey, warranties from an environmental consultant, etc) or make due enquiries of a vendor to ensure it has adequate protection. A landlord who baulks at a clause like this should be put to proof as to what he knows about the site which causes him to reject the principle.

INSURANCE

5.1 It may simply not be possible for a tenant to know all of the convictions, judgments, etc which may exist against all the people listed. If a company is a shareholder of the corporate tenant what steps must the tenant take to pierce the corporate veil? The amendment seeks to reflect this.

5.2 The first amendment is in square brackets because, in this scenario, it is extremely unlikely a landlord would accept it. It would not be practical for the landlord to insure a multi-tenanted building in various names. The best such a tenant is likely to get is a note of his interest being made on the policy (see new clause 5.9.2). As in clause 4.2.1, the original drafting here seeks to impose a precondition to the landlord's covenant to insure. The same arguments apply here as those stated above in relation to clause 4.2.1. The second amendment provides that the tenant is not responsible for any member of the general public who enters the premises as licensee, contractor, statutory undertaker, etc. The additional (and in the author's view essential) element of control seeks, at least, to restrict the category of persons who can vitiate the insurance and to make the clause more objective and better balanced.

5.3 Details of the insurance

5.3.1 Office, underwriters and agency

Insurance is to be effected in such reputable and substantial insurance office in the UK or whose principal office is in the UK, or with such underwriters, and through such reputable and substantial agency as the Landlord (acting reasonably) from time to time decides

5.3.2 Insurance cover

Insurance must be effected for the following amounts:

5.3.2.1 the reasonable and proper sum that the Landlord is from time to time advised by his Surveyor is the full cost of rebuilding and reinstating the Building, including ~~VAT~~ architects', surveyors', engineers', solicitors' and all other professional persons' fees, the fees payable on any applications for planning permission or other permits or consents that may be required in relation to rebuilding or reinstating the Building, the reasonable and proper cost of preparation of the site including shoring-up, debris removal, demolition, site clearance and any works that may be required by statute, and incidental expenses and

5.3.2.2 loss of rental and service charge income from the Building, taking account of any rent review that may be due, for 3 years or such longer period as the Landlord from time to time reasonably requires for planning and carrying out the rebuilding or reinstatement

5.3.3 Risks insured

Insurance must be effected against damage or destruction by any of the Insured Risks to the extent that such insurance may ordinarily be arranged with a substantial and reputable insurer for properties such as the Building, subject to such excesses, exclusions or limitations as the insurer requires

5.4 Payment of the Insurance Rent

The Tenant covenants to pay the Insurance Rent for the period starting on the commencement date of the Term and ending on the day before the next policy renewal date on the date of this document, and subsequently to pay the Insurance Rent on demand ~~and, if so demanded, in advance of the policy renewal date~~

5.5 Suspension of the Rent

5.5.1 Events giving rise to suspension

If and whenever the Building or any part of it or any access way or ways (or any part of them) to it or any essential services to it is or

5.3.1 This amendment is self-explanatory and seeks to ensure that as much as possible is done by the landlord to ensure that, should there ever be a need to claim under the insurance policy, the insurance company has not disappeared. By stipulating the UK it will be easier to trace what has happened, if anything untoward has indeed happened. The final element to the amendment seeks to ensure that once again there is an element of objectivity as to which insurance office, underwriters or agency the landlord chooses to insure through.

5.3.2.1 The first amendment to this clause seeks to ensure that the landlord does not over- or under-insure and, once again, brings the surveyor into play to exercise his professional judgement in a proper and ethical manner. Reference to VAT has been deleted on the basis that the additional expense of insuring against any VAT which may be payable on any reinstatement costs will not be justified if the landlord has opted to tax and is able to recover that VAT. The final amendment brings into play an objective element as regards costs.

5.3.2.2 This amendment is self-explanatory, bringing into play an element of reasonableness.

5.3.3 This amendment ties in the landlord's covenant with the obligation contained in clause 5.3.1.

5.4 The deletion at the end of this clause ensures that it is only once the policy premium demand is made by the insurance company that the tenant is obliged to reimburse. As has been stated earlier (see clause 1.16), the rationale behind insurance rent is simply that it is a *reimbursement* of monies laid out by the landlord.

5.5.1 The first amendment seeks to ensure that, if the premises remain undamaged but are inaccessible or unusable because of damage to access ways or corridors or other means of access or essential services then, even though in strict terms the premises are not damaged, since they are damaged or destroyed by one or more of the Insured Risks or otherwise except one against which insurance may not ordinarily be arranged with a substantial and reputable insurer for properties such as the Building unless the Landlord has in fact insured against that risk so that the Premises are unfit for immediate occupation and or use by the Tenant , and payment of the save to the extent that insurance money is not wholly or partly refused by reason because of any act or default of the Tenant or anyone at the Building expressly or by implication with his authority and under his control then the provisions of clause 5.5.2 SUSPENDING THE RENT are to have effect

5.5.2 Suspending the Rent

In the circumstances mentioned in clause 5.5.1 EVENTS GIVING RISE TO SUSPENSION, the Lease Rents and the Service Charge or a fair proportion of the Lease Rents and the Service Charge according to the nature and the extent of the damage sustained, is to cease to be payable until the Building or access way or ways have has been rebuilt or reinstated so as to render the Premises fit for immediate occupation and use by the Tenant, or until the end of 3 years from the destruction or damage whichever period is the shorter, the proportion of the Lease Rents and the Service Charge suspended and any dispute as to the proportion of the Rent suspended and the period of the suspension to be determined in accordance with the Arbitration Act 1996 by an arbitrator to be appointed by agreement between the Landlord and the Tenant or in default by the President or other proper officer for the time being of the Royal Institution of Chartered Surveyors upon the application of either the Landlord or the Tenant

5.6 Reinstatement and termination

5.6.1 Obligation to obtain permissions

If and whenever the Building or any part of it is or any access way or ways or any essential services to it are damaged or destroyed by one or more of the Insured Risks except one against which insurance may not ordinarily be arranged with a substantial and reputable insurer for properties such as the Building unless the Landlord has in fact insured against that risk, and payment of the insurance money is not wholly or partly refused because of any act or default of the Tenant or anyone at the Building expressly or by implication with his authority and under his control then the Landlord must use reasonable best endeavours to obtain any planning permissions or other permits and consents ('permissions') that are required under the Planning Acts or otherwise to enable him to rebuild and reinstate the Building or the access way or ways or any essential services cannot be used by the tenant the rent suspension provisions will, nevertheless, kick in. The other amendments to the clause narrow down the circumstances where the rent suspension will cease to operate so that the tenant could be required to commence rental payments again. The damage or destruction may not simply be as a result of an Insured Risk. In our lease here we need to focus on the fact that a particular tenant is occupying particular premises and, therefore, those premises must be suitable for his immediate needs; hence the amendment to ensure that the premises must be made fit for immediate use and occupation by the specific tenant before that tenant becomes liable to pay rent again. As originally drafted the clause makes the tenant liable for the entire consequences of insurance vitiation even if only part of the insurance monies have been refused and the penultimate amendment seeks to deal with that. The final amendment is restrictive once again in the tenant's favour so that the tenant is not responsible for the acts anyone on the premises with authority but over whom the tenant has no control.

5.5.2 The first amendment to this clause seeks to ensure that it is not only the rent (as defined in clause 1.34) which is suspended but also the Insurance Rent (as defined) and service charge payments which may be due and owing. It is manifestly unfair for a tenant to have to pay any of these items if his premises are unusable. The balance of the amendments are included for the same reasons as referred to in clause 5.5.1. A final point to bear in mind in relation to this clause relates to the limitation period for which payment of rent by virtue of the insurance policy subsists. Ideally there should be no time limit expressed but if there is one it should tie in with the time period within which the tenant can terminate the lease and walk away (see clause 5.6.4 as amended) because, theoretically at least, at the end of the stated three year period the tenant could become contractually liable to pay the rent etc again. A tenant would not thank his advisers if all that was left was the nebulous and undecided '*frustration*' argument.

5.6.1 The same rationale applies here in respect of the proposed amendments as that referred to in clause 5.5.1 above.

5.6.2 Obligation to reinstate

Subject to the provisions of clause 5.6.3 RELIEF FROM THE OBLIGATION TO REINSTATE, and, if any permissions are required, after they have been obtained, the Landlord must as soon as reasonably practicable apply all money received in respect of such insurance (except sums in respect of loss of the Rent) making up any shortfall out of its own monies in rebuilding or reinstating the parts of the Building and for the access way or ways destroyed or damaged

5.6.3 Relief from the obligation to reinstate

The Landlord need not rebuild or reinstate the Building if and for so long as the rebuilding or reinstating is prevented because:

5.6.3.1 the Landlord, despite using ~~reasonable~~ best endeavours, cannot obtain a necessary permission

5.6.3.2 any permission is granted subject to a lawful condition with which in all the circumstances it is unreasonable to expect the Landlord to comply because the cost in so doing would be out of all proportion to the cost of otherwise rebuilding or reinstating

5.6.3.3 there is some defect or deficiency in the site on which the rebuilding or reinstatement is to take place that means it can only be undertaken at a cost that is unreasonable in all the circumstances

5.6.3.4 the Landlord is unable to obtain access to the site to rebuild or reinstate

5.6.3.5 the rebuilding or reinstating is prevented by war, act of God, government action, ~~strike or lock-out~~ or

because of the occurrence of any other circumstances beyond the Landlord's reasonable control

5.6.4 Notice to terminate

If the Premises are still not fit for the Tenant's immediate occupation and use or the access way or ways or essential services have not been reinstated so that at the end of a period of ~~3~~ 2 years and 9 months starting on the date of the damage or destruction, ~~the Landlord~~ either party may by notice served on the ~~Tenant~~ other at any time ~~within 6 months of~~ after the end of that period ('a notice to terminate following failure to reinstate') implement the provisions of clause 5.6.5 TERMINATION FOLLOWING FAILURE TO REINSTATE

5.6.2 The first amendment ensures that if, for whatever reason, the landlord has not insured for the full reinstatement value, then the tenant is not penalised. Without this amendment if there is a shortfall then the premises may end up only partially reinstated. This amendment seeks to ensure that, if nothing else, at least the landlord will take great care to ensure that he has sufficient insurance cover in place so that he doesn't have to fund any shortfall himself. In any event the tenant will be funding the insurance premium via the insurance rent so it is difficult to see any sort of sustainable argument on the part of the landlord as to why this amendment should not be included and the tenant should hold out for this amendment.

5.6.3.1 Certain cases have suggested that there is little practical difference between a covenant to use 'best endeavours', a covenant to use 'reasonable endeavours' and a covenant to 'take all reasonable steps'. However, the decision in *UBH (Mechanical Services) Ltd v Standard Life Assurance Co* (1986) Times, 13 November, indicates that the latter two forms of obligation may mean something less than 'best' endeavours. The author contends that this is one of the circumstances where there has to be an obligation on the landlord to use best (as opposed to anything else) endeavours because the tenant is threatened with losing his interest in the premises which, by reason of its location or otherwise, may be critical to his business.

5.6.3.2 The amendment at the end of this clause is self-explanatory and seeks to define and limit the circumstances in which the provisions would apply.

5.6.3.5 It is the author's view that strike or lockout can in many instances with appropriate steps on the landlord's part be prevented. These are political matters for the landlord to resolve and are, at least on most occasions of a short-term nature only and within the sphere of influence of the landlord. The other items listed are conceded as being outside his control!

5.6.4 The amendments here provide that it is not only the landlord who has the ability to terminate the lease if there is a delay in reinstating the premises accessways or services such that the tenant cannot have back what was granted to him by the lease. It is the author's view that of the two parties the landlord is the one most likely to want to reinstate the premises, reinstate the tenant and ensure his investment retained its value. However, clearly, the tenant himself has business needs which will need to be satisfied and the tenant will not be in a position to wait around indefinitely while the landlord decides whether or not to obtain the relevant permissions and reinstate the premises. The time periods attempt to dovetail together to ensure that during the period of rent suspension there is no chance of the landlord calling upon the tenant to recommence rental payments. Ideally speaking, once the premises have been badly damaged or destroyed the tenant may want to have the ability to walk away and relocate almost immediately rather than wait for a considerable period while the premises are reinstated. If this is the case then a shorter period than that currently specified in clause 5.6.4 should be negotiated.

5.6.5 Termination following failure to reinstate

On service of a notice to terminate following failure to reinstate, the Term is to cease absolutely but without prejudice to any rights or remedies that may have accrued and all money received in respect of the insurance effected by the Landlord pursuant to this Lease is to be divided between the parties according to the relative value of their estates in the Premises ~~belong to the Landlord absolutely~~

5.7 Tenant's further insurance covenants

The Tenant covenants with the Landlord to observe and perform the requirements contained in this clause 5.7

5.7.1 Requirements of insurers

The Tenant must comply with all the reasonable requirements and recommendations of the insurers of which he has written notice

5.7.2 Policy avoidance and additional premiums

The Tenant must not knowingly do or omit anything that could cause any insurance policy on or in relation to the Building to become wholly or partly void or voidable, or do or omit anything by which additional insurance premiums may become payable unless he has previously notified the Landlord and has agreed to pay the increased premium

5.7.3 Fire-fighting equipment

The Tenant must keep the Premises supplied with such fire fighting equipment as the insurers and~~,~~ the fire authority require and the Landlord reasonably requires and must maintain the equipment to the reasonable satisfaction of the insurers and the fire authority and in efficient working order. ~~At least once in every 6 months period~~ As often as reasonably necessary the Tenant must have the sprinkler system and other fire fighting equipment inspected by a competent person

5.7.4 Combustible materials

The Tenant must not store on the Premises or bring onto them anything of a specially combustible, inflammable or explosive nature, and must comply with the requirements and recommendations of the fire authority and the reasonable requirements of the Landlord as to fire precautions relating to the Premises

5.7.5 Fire escapes, equipment and doors

The Tenant must not obstruct the access to any fire equipment or the means of escape from the Premises or lock any fire door while the Premises are occupied

5.6.5 There has been much academic debate and some case law (*Beacon Carpets Ltd v Kirby* [1985] QB 755, CA) over the years (both inside and outside the court) as to whom insurance monies in this situation belong. On a fairly lengthy lease (eg prime retail space) there is likely to be some value in the tenant's interest and there is no sustainable reason, in the author's view, why the tenant should not benefit in some way, shape or form from the insurance monies. While the method of valuing the tenant's interest is likely to prove contentious, the principle of division of insurance monies between the parties is a fair one.

5.7.1 It is unreasonable to expect a tenant to comply with requirements and recommendations of which it has no notice and which may be unreasonable either on their own account or in cost terms, and the amendments reflect these factors.

5.7.2 This small amendment imparts the pressure of knowledge to ensure that the tenant is not strictly liable for an event or occurrence of which he is not aware.

5.7.3 The amendments here introduce the concept of reasonableness in relation to the landlord's requirements only. The final amendment brings an element of flexibility and objectivity into what otherwise is a fixed and unforgiving timetable.

5.7.4 This amendment seeks to ensure that the concept of reasonableness applies in relation to the landlord's requirements.

5.7.6 Notice of events affecting the policy

As soon as reasonably practicable after becoming aware of the same ~~T~~the Tenant must give ~~immediate~~ notice to the Landlord of any event of which he is aware that might affect any insurance policy on or relating to the Premises, and of any event against which the Landlord may have insured under this Lease

5.7.7 Notice of convictions

As soon as reasonably practicable after becoming aware of the same ~~T~~the Tenant must give ~~immediate~~ notice to the Landlord of any conviction, judgment or finding of any court or tribunal relating to the Tenant, or any director other officer or major shareholder of the Tenant, of such a nature as to be likely to affect the decision of any insurer or underwriter to grant or to continue any insurance of the Premises

5.7.8 Other insurance

If at any time the Tenant is entitled to the benefit of any insurance of the Premises that is not effected or maintained in pursuance of any obligation contained in this Lease, the Tenant must apply all money received by virtue of such insurance in making good the loss or damage in respect of which the money is received

5.8 Increase or decrease of the Building

5.8.1 Variation of the Insurance Rent Percentage

If the size of the Building is permanently increased or decreased, the Insurance Rent Percentage may be varied, if the Landlord reasonably so requires, with effect from the date of any consequent alteration in the Insurance Rent

5.8.2 Determination of the variation

The amount by which the Insurance Rent Percentage is varied is to be agreed by the Landlord and the Tenant or, in default of agreement within 2 months of the first proposal for variation made by the Landlord, is to be the amount the Surveyor, acting reasonably and as an expert and not as an arbitrator, determines to be fair and reasonable

5.9 Landlord's Additional Insurance Covenants

The Landlord covenants with the Tenant to observe and perform the requirements set out in this clause 5.9 in relation to the insurance policy he has effected pursuant to his obligations contained in this Lease

5.7.6 This amendment is self-explanatory. Again, without it, the strict liability imposed by the clause may work against the tenant at some future date.

5.7.7 The first amendment again avoids the imposition of a strict liability timetable. The second amendment makes the clause specific to the insurance of the premises in question.

5.8.1 The amendment proposed here introduces the concept of reasonableness into the landlord's decision to alter the percentages. An alternative would be to provide for this decision to be made by the surveyor if no clause such as 5.8.2 was included in the original draft lease.

5.8.2 In the absence of agreement on the varied Insurance Rent Percentage the ultimate arbiter will be the surveyor, acting reasonably.

5.9 (new) This new clause imposes important obligations on the landlord very much in the interests of the tenant such as ensuring that the tenant is kept abreast of changes relating to the insurance policy. If the insurance is in the joint names of the landlord and the tenant or the tenant's interest is noted on the policy the waiver of subrogation referred to in clause 5.9.4 will most likely not be needed. If not, and the tenant damages the premises through lack of care, he runs the risk of being sued by the landlord's insurer under the doctrine of subrogation (although there is case law to support the argument that when a tenant reimburses the landlord the cost of the insurance subrogation cannot apply (*Mark Rowlands Ltd v Berni Inns Ltd* [1986] QB 211, CA) but this case was expressed to turn on stated facts and cannot be regarded as fixing a principle). Clearly, however, obtaining the sort of letter referred to in clause 5.9.4 put the matter beyond doubt.

5.9.1 Copy Policy

The Landlord must produce to the Tenant on demand a copy of the policy and the last premium renewal receipt

5.9.2 Noting of the Tenant's interest

The Landlord must ensure that the interest of the Tenant is noted or endorsed on the policy

5.9.3 Change of risks

The Landlord must notify the Tenant of any material change in the risks covered by the policy from time to time

5.9.4 Waiver of subrogation

The Landlord must produce to the Tenant on demand written confirmation from the insurers that they have agreed to waive all rights of subrogation against the Tenant]

6 GUARANTEE PROVISIONS

6.1 The Guarantors Covenants

6.1.1 Nature and duration

The Guarantor's covenants with the Landlord are given ~~as sole or principal debtor or covenantor,~~ with the landlord for the time being and with all his successors in title without the need for any express assignment, and the Guarantor's obligations to the Landlord will last throughout the Liability Period

6.1.2 The covenants

The Guarantor covenants with the Landlord to observe the requirements of this clause 6.1.2

6.1.2.1 Payment of rent and performance of the Lease

The Tenant must pay the Lease Rents and (upon receipt of a valid VAT invoice addressed to the Tenant for the full amount) VAT charged on them punctually and observe and perform the covenants and other terms of this Lease, and if, at any time during the Liability Period while the Tenant is bound by the tenant covenants of this Lease, the Tenant defaults in paying the Lease Rents or in observing or performing any of the covenants or other terms of this Lease, then the Guarantor must upon receipt of a valid VAT invoice addressed to the Tenant for the full amount pay the Lease Rents and observe or perform the covenants or terms in respect of which the Tenant is

6 GUARANTEE PROVISIONS

It is important to consider, in the context of the requirement for a guarantor, whether as legal adviser acting on behalf of a tenant, there is any potential conflict of interest in representing a guarantor also and, if so, whether the guarantor should be told to seek independent legal advice.

6.1 The deletion here ensures that the *guarantee* takes effect only as a guarantee and not as a principal indemnity. While a detailed discussion of the difference between a guarantee and an indemnity is beyond the scope of this book, briefly, a primary indemnity takes effect as a direct primary promise to pay what is owing and not simply an undertaking to pay if the tenant fails to pay. In simple terms a primary indemnity puts the guarantor in a position comparable to that of an original tenant.

6.1.2.1 This amendment is necessary to achieve consistency with the VAT provisions inserted elsewhere throughout the lease. The final amendment removes the obligation to indemnity for reasons explained in clause 3.14 (deleted).

in default and make good to the Landlord on demand~~, and indemnify the Landlord against,~~ all reasonably foreseeable Losses resulting from such non-payment, non-performance or non-observance notwithstanding:

6.1.2.1.1 any time or indulgence granted by the Landlord to the Tenant, any neglect or forbearance of the Landlord in enforcing the payment of the Lease Rents or the observance or performance of the covenants or other terms of this Lease, or any refusal by the Landlord to accept rent tendered by or on behalf of the Tenant at a time when the Landlord is entitled (or will after the service of a notice under the Law of Property Act 1925 section 146 be entitled) to re-enter the Premises

6.1.2.1.2 that the terms of this Lease may have been varied by agreement between the Landlord and the Tenant (provided that no such variation is to bind the Guarantor to the extent that it is prejudicial to him)

6.1.2.1.3 that the Tenant has surrendered part of the Premises—in which event the liability of the Guarantor under this Lease is to continue in respect of the part of the Premises not surrendered after making any necessary apportionments under the Law of Property Act 1925 section 140, and

6.1.2.1.4 anything else by which, but for this clause 6.1.2.1, the Guarantor would be released

6.1.2.2 New lease following disclaimer

If, at any time during the Liability Period while the Tenant is bound by the tenant covenants of this Lease, any trustee in bankruptcy or liquidator of the Tenant disclaims this Lease, the Guarantor must, if reasonably so required by notice served by the Landlord within 28 ~~60~~ days of the Landlord's becoming aware of the disclaimer, take from the Landlord forthwith a lease of the Premises for the residue of the Contractual Term as at the date of the disclaimer, at the Rent then payable under this Lease and subject to the same covenants and terms as in this Lease the new lease to commence on the date of the disclaimer. The Guarantor must pay the reasonable and proper costs of the new lease and VAT charged thereon, save where such VAT is recoverable or available for set off by the Landlord as input tax, and execute and deliver to the Landlord a counterpart of the new lease

6.1.2.3 Payments following disclaimer

If this Lease is disclaimed and the Landlord does not require the Guarantor to accept a new lease of the Premises in accordance with clause 6.1.2.2 NEW LEASE FOLLOWING DISCLAIMER, the Guarantor must pay to the Landlord ~~on~~ as soon as reasonably practicable following demand an amount equal to the difference between any money received by the Landlord for the use or occupation of the Premises and the Lease Rents for the period commencing with the date of the disclaimer and ending on whichever is the earlier of the date being ~~6~~ 3 months after the disclaimer or the date, if any, upon

6.1.2.1.2 It is important that any variation agreed between landlord and tenant is not prejudicial to the guarantor. While prior to the Landlord and Tenant (Covenants) Act 1995 the basic rule of law was that a guarantor would be released from his liability by any change (variation) in the principal contract (the lease) between the landlord and the tenant (except in relation to an immaterial variation or a variation for the guarantor's benefit), section 18 of the Landlord and Tenant (Covenants) Act 1995 has now altered that basic rule for any variation taking effect after 1 January 1995 (for either old or new leases). Now the guarantee remains in place but the Act imposes a limit on the responsibility of the guarantor by stripping away any liability which arises in consequence of the variation.

6.1.2.2 While the author has added the word *reasonably* it is unlikely there are going to be any circumstances when it would be unreasonable for the landlord to request this. However, there is always the remote possibility that this may be the case and this argument should be used against the landlord for its inclusion. Shortening the time period attempts to bring matters to a head so that the guarantor, at least, knows exactly where he stands within a relatively short period, ie is he going to be asked to take on board a new lease or not? The amendment relating to the costs of the new lease is self-explanatory as is the inclusion of the wording relating to VAT.

6.1.2.3 The first amendment is self-explanatory and attempts to ensure that no undue financial burden is placed on the guarantor in terms of cash flow (if nothing else), while the second obliges the landlord to bring into account any monies received in respect of the premises (ie mitigating his loss) thereby reducing the tenant's liability. The reduction of the time period from six to three months imposes a more reasonable period for the ongoing liability. The final amendment imposes an obligation on the landlord to mitigate his loss. Such an obligation may be unacceptable to a landlord in the context of a tenant breach and perhaps a '*reasonable endeavours*' obligation would be an acceptable compromise.

which the Premises are relet (which the Landlord covenants to use its best endeavours to do), and the end of the Contractual Term

~~**6.1.2.4 Guarantee of the Tenant's liabilities under an authorised guarantee agreement**~~

~~If, at any time during the Liability Period while the Tenant is bound by an authorised guarantee agreement, the Tenant makes any default in his obligations under that agreement, the Guarantor must make good to the Landlord on demand, and indemnify the Landlord against, all Losses resulting from that default notwithstanding:~~

~~6.1.2.4.1 any time or indulgence granted by the Landlord to the Tenant, or neglect or forbearance of the Landlord in enforcing the payment of any sum or the observance or performance of the covenants of the authorised guarantee agreement~~

~~6.1.2.4.2 that the terms of the authorised guarantee agreement may have been varied by agreement between the Landlord and the Tenant~~

~~6.1.2.4.3 anything else by which, but for this clause 6.1.2.4, the Guarantor would be released~~

6.1.3 Severance

6.1.3.1 Severance of void provisions

Any provision of this clause 6 rendered void by virtue of the 1995 Act section 25 is to be severed from all remaining provisions, and the remaining provisions are to be preserved

6.1.3.2 Limitation of provisions

If any provision in this clause 6 extends beyond the limits permitted by the 1995 Act section 25, that provision is to be varied so as not to extend beyond those limits

6.2 The Landlord's Covenant

The Landlord covenants with the Guarantor that he will not attempt or be entitled to recover from the Guarantor any payment of any amount, determined by a court or in binding arbitration or agreed between the Landlord and the Tenant, payable in respect of a breach of covenant by the Tenant, unless he has served on the Guarantor, within 6 months of the payment being determined or agreed, a notice in the form prescribed by section 27 of the 1995 Act as if the payment were a fixed charge under that Act

6.1.2.4 There is a healthy academic debate going on at the moment (and still unresolved) as to whether or not section 25 of the Landlord and Tenant (Covenants) Act 1995 precludes the landlord from requiring a guarantor of an original tenant or assignee under a lease to act as a guarantor of the original tenant or who enters into an authorised guarantee agreement. For what it is worth it is the author's view that section 25 does preclude this requirement and, therefore, the author's view is that this clause should be deleted in its entirety. If the landlord's argument and bargaining position, however, win the day then, pending a decision of the courts on this point, the tenant's adviser should seek to ensure that similar amendments are made to this clause as those contained in clause 6.1.2.1.

6.2 (new) This amendment is self-explanatory and, in effect, inserts as a contractual obligation the provisions contained in section 27 of the Landlord and Tenant (Covenants) Act 1995.

7 FORFEITURE

If and whenever during the Term:

7.1 ~~the~~any undisputed ~~Lease~~ Rents~~, or any of them or any part of them, or any VAT payable on them, are~~ is outstanding for ~~14~~28 days after becoming due, whether formally demanded or not or

7.2 the Tenant or the Guarantor materially breaches any covenant or other term of this Lease or

7.3 the Tenant or the Guarantor, being an individual, becomes bankrupt or

7.4 the Tenant or the Guarantor, being a company, enters into liquidation whether compulsory or voluntary (but not if the liquidation is for amalgamation or reconstruction of a solvent company) or has a receiver appointed or

7.5 the Tenant enters into an arrangement for the benefit of his creditors or

7.6 the Tenant has any distress or execution levied on his goods at the Premises

and, where the Tenant or the Guarantor is more than one person, if and whenever any of the events referred to in this clause happens to any one or more of them the Landlord may at any time re-enter the Premises or any part of them in the name of the whole—even if any previous right of re-entry has been waived and thereupon the Term is to cease absolutely but without prejudice to any rights or remedies that may have accrued to ~~the Landlord against the Tenant or the Guarantor~~ any party other than in respect of any breach of covenant or other term of this Lease, including the breach in respect of which the re-entry is made

7 FORFEITURE

It may well be that landlords and their advisers are reluctant to accept any form of amendment to this particular clause but this does not mean that the tenant's adviser should not at least attempt to insert some amendments.

7.1 There may clearly be a case where rental payments (or other payments if the landlord will not accept the deletion) due under the lease are, in fact, disputed for one reason or another. The first amendment deals with that situation (disputes are unlikely to arise in relation to fixed sums which are set out in the lease or in a rent review memorandum following a review of the rent but more likely to arise in relation to service charge payments or insurance rent payments which are not fixed). The second amendment ensures that any period of grace within which payment can be made (see clause 3.17) is consistent with the timescale set out in this clause.

7.2 The amendment here is self-explanatory and prevents the landlord from harassing the tenant by instigating forfeiture proceedings for immaterial breaches. It may also be worth amending all references in the forfeiture clause to '*the Tenant*' to read '*the current tenant of the premises* ...'. This would ensure that any attempt by a landlord to argue for forfeiture on the ground of eg liquidation of a previous corporate tenant would fail.

7.4 There may be good corporate re-organisational reasons why it is necessary for a solvent corporate tenant to be amalgamated in some way, shape or form. The amendment inserted here prevents the landlord from using this as an opportunity to claim forfeiture of the lease.

7.6 It may well be that a third party may seek to distrain on goods as a result of a dispute that has nothing to do with the landlord and tenant relationship at this particular premises, for example where there is a dispute between the tenant and his landlord at another premises. The amendment seeks to ensure that it is only distress executed in relation to goods stored at the subject premises that will give rise to the right to forfeiture.

The final amendment preserves any accrued rights and remedies of either party against the other party or parties since the original wording only preserves the position of the landlord against the tenant and guarantor when there may well be claims by the tenant and/or the guarantor against the landlord which must also be taken into account.

8 MISCELLANEOUS

8.1 Exclusion of warranty as to use

Nothing in this Lease or in any consent granted by the Landlord under this Lease is to imply or warrant that the Premises may lawfully be used under the Planning Acts as offices

8.2 Representations

The Tenant acknowledges that this Lease has not been entered into wholly or partly in reliance on any statement or representation made by or on behalf of the Landlord except any such statement or representation expressly set out in this Lease and in any written or other replies made by the Landlord's Solicitors of any enquiries raised by the Tenant's solicitor

8.3 Documents under hand

While the Landlord is a limited company or other corporation, any licence, consent, approval or notice required to be given by the Landlord ~~is to be sufficiently given if given under the hand of a director, the secretary or other duly authorised officer of the Landlord or by the Surveyor on behalf of the Landlord~~must be given as a deed properly executed by the Landlord

8.4 Tenant's property

If, after the Tenant has vacated the Premises at the end of the Term any property of his remains in or on the Premises and he fails to remove it within ~~7~~14 days after a written request from the Landlord to do so or, if the Landlord is unable to make such a request to the Tenant despite having used his best endeavours so to do, within ~~14~~28 days from the first attempt to make one, then the Landlord may sell that property as the agent of the Tenant. ~~The Tenant must indemnify the Landlord against any liability incurred by the Landlord to any third party whose property is sold by him in the mistaken belief held in good faith—which is to be presumed unless the contrary is proved—that the property belonged to the Tenant~~. If, having used its best~~made reasonable~~ efforts to do so, the Landlord is unable to locate the Tenant, then the Landlord may retain the proceeds of sale absolutely unless the Tenant claims them within 6 months of the date upon which he vacated the Premises. ~~The Tenant must indemnify the Landlord against any damage occasioned to the Premises and any losses caused by or related to the presence of the property in or on the Premises~~

8 MISCELLANEOUS

8.2 This is a standard amendment familiar to conveyancers in any form of property-based contractual relationship and it is unlikely to prove to be contentious.

8.3 If the landlord is a corporate body then there should be no room for dispute as to whether the signatory to a document has been duly authorised or whether for any other reason the document has been validly executed. This amendment seeks to avoid this. While there may be delays occasioned by relevant signatories etc not being available, it is far preferable to have a delay prior to execution of the documentation rather than problems later if the landlord so seeks to argue that the document executed under hand was signed by an individual who did not have the requisite authority.

8.4 From the tenant's point of view, ideally this entire clause should be deleted. It is unlikely that any tenant is going to disappear completely without trace. A corporate tenant is nearly always traceable either through a liquidator, receiver or other officers although, admittedly, it may be more difficult with individuals who choose for whatever reasons to go missing. In any event, if the goods belong to the tenant then the landlord should try to return them. However, a landlord is not likely to want to be in a position whereby at the end of the term he cannot re-let the premises because the previous tenant's goods are still located there. If deletion of the whole clause proves to be unacceptable the suggested amendments should be sought. The time periods are self-explanatory as is the provision imposing an obligation on the landlord to try and locate the tenant. The reason for deletion of the indemnities has been discussed in clause 3.12.1.

8.5 Compensation on vacating excluded

~~Any statutory right of the Tenant to claim compensation from the Landlord on vacating the Premises is excluded to the extent that the law allows~~

8.6 Notices

8.6.1 Form and service of notices

A notice under this Lease must be in writing and, unless the receiving party or his authorised agent acknowledges receipt, is valid if, and only if:

8.6.1.1 it is given by hand, sent by registered post or recorded delivery~~, or sent by fax provided a confirmatory copy is given by hand or sent by registered post or recorded delivery on the same day~~ and

8.6.1.2 it is served:

8.6.1.2.1 where the receiving party is a company incorporated within Great Britain, at the registered office

8.6.1.2.2 where the receiving party is the Tenant and the Tenant is not such a company, at the Premises and

8.6.1.2.3 where the receiving party is the Landlord or the Guarantor and that party is not such a company, at that party's address shown in this Lease or at any address specified in a notice given by that party to the other parties

8.6.2 Deemed delivery

8.6.2.1 By registered post or recorded delivery

Unless it is returned through the Royal Mail undelivered, a notice sent by registered post or recorded delivery is to be treated as served on the 2nd working day after posting whenever, and whether or not, it is received

~~**8.6.2.2 By fax**~~

~~A notice sent by fax is to be treated as served on the day on which it is sent, or the next working day where the fax is sent after 1600 hours or on a day that is not a working day, whenever and whether or not it or the confirmatory copy is received unless the confirmatory copy is returned through the Royal Mail undelivered~~

8.6.2.3 'A working day'

References to 'a working day' are references to a day when the majority of the United Kingdom clearing banks are open for business in the City of London

8.5 If there has been a change of ownership of the lease during the last five years of the contractual term and any assignee is *not* a successor to the business of the assignor (and possibly previous occupier) the landlord is able, contractually, in the lease to delay statutory compensation to the tenant. The author regards this as unsustainable from the landlord's point of view and should be strenuously resisted by the tenant. Such a provision as originally drafted may affect marketability of the lease in its last five years.

8.6.1 Insertion of the word '*authorised*' seeks to ensure that there is no dispute as to whether or not the party acknowledging receipt of the notice had the necessary authority to do so.

8.6.1.1 There is always a potential debate as to whether or not a notice sent by fax has in fact actually been received and, if received, what has been done with it at the receiving address. Was it brought to the attention of the appropriate person? Was it simply left on someone's desk date stamped and then mislaid? It is better to be safe and provide for more traditional methods of service.

8.6.2.2 The same comments apply here as that referred to in clause 8.6.1.1 above.

8.6.2.3 The amendment here is self-explanatory.

8.6.3 Joint recipients

If the receiving party consists of more than one person, a notice to one of them is notice to all

8.7 Rights and easements

The operation of the Law of Property Act 1925 section 62 is excluded from this Lease and the only rights granted to the Tenant are those expressly set out in this Lease and the Tenant is not to be entitled to any other rights affecting any adjoining property of the Landlord

8.8 Covenants relating to adjoining property

~~The Tenant is not to be entitled to the benefit of or the right to enforce or to prevent the release or modification of any covenant agreement or condition entered into by any tenant of the Landlord in respect of any adjoining property of the Landlord~~

8.9 Disputes with adjoining occupiers

If any dispute arises between the Tenant and the tenants or occupiers of any adjoining property of the Landlord in connection with the Premises and any of that adjoining property, it is to be decided by the ~~Landlord~~ Surveyor or in such other manner as the Landlord reasonably directs

8.10 Effect of waiver

~~Each of the Tenant's covenants is to remain in full force both at law and in equity even if the Landlord has waived or released that covenant, or waived or released any similar covenant affecting any adjoining property of the Landlord~~

8.11 The perpetuity period

The perpetuity period applicable to this Lease is 80 years from the commencement of the Contractual Term, and whenever in this Lease any party is granted a future interest it must vest within that period or be void for remoteness

8.12 Exclusion of liability

~~The Landlord is not to be responsible to the Tenant or to anyone at the Premises or the Estate expressly or by implication with the Tenant's authority for any accident happening or injury suffered or for any damage to or loss of any chattel sustained in the Premises or on the Estate~~

8.8 Consideration should be given as to whether this clause should be deleted by the tenant's adviser after ascertaining whether such covenants exist and, if so, does the tenant need the benefit of them. There are only a limited set of circumstances in which one tenant may be able to enforce a covenant against another (a building scheme, a letting scheme, where tenants (or their predecessors) have entered into a mutual deed of covenant or where a tenant has taken an assignment of the benefit of a covenant from the landlord) and it is unlikely a commercial lease will fall into any of these categories. If the landlord insists that the clause remains, a proviso should be added at the end as follows, '... *provided always that the Premises are not adversely affected thereby*'.

8.9 The amendment provides an element of professional expertise is brought to bear and the concept of reasonableness is introduced in any such disputes. The tenant needs to be aware that this clause may restrict any independent action it may wish to take against another tenant and the tenant may wish to see this clause deleted. It will only be enforceable, if it remains, if the other tenant who is party to the dispute has a similar provision in his clause.

8.10 This clause attempts to get round the harsh application of the law of waiver. As the law stands at present it is the author's view that this clause is void and should be deleted.

8.11 The amendment at the end of the clause spells out the effect of a failure of a future right to vest within the perpetuity period.

8.12 The author would press for this clause to be deleted in its entirety. It is not possible to *contract out* of liability for negligence resulting in personal injury, or death and the tenant should argue that the clause should be deleted on this basis. Alternatively, the tenant's adviser should seek to turn it around and impose a reciprocal exclusion on the landlord so that neither party is responsible to the other for the consequences of any of the matters set out in this clause and then leave it for the courts to decide the extent to which such exclusions are effective.

8.13 New lease

This lease is a new tenancy for the purposes of the 1995 Act section 1

8.14 Agreement for lease

It is certified that there is no agreement for lease to which this documents gives effect

8.15 Exclusion of the 1954 Act ss 24–28

Pursuant to the authorisation by an order of the Stoke-on-Trent County Court made on the day of 1998 under the provisions of the Landlord and Tenant Act 1954 section 38(4) (as amended by the Law of Property Act 1969 section 5) the parties agree that the provisions of sections 24–28 inclusive of the 1954 Act are excluded in relation to the tenancy created by this Lease

8.16 Tenants Break Clause

If the Tenant wishes to determine this lease on the day of and shall give to the Landlord not less than [ ] months notice in writing and shall up to the time of such determination pay the rent reserved by ~~and perform and observe the covenants contracted in this~~ Lease then upon the expiry of such notice the Term shall immediately cease and determine but without prejudice to any rights ~~the Landlord~~ <u>either party</u> may have against the ~~Tenant~~ <u>other</u> for any antecedent breach

IN WITNESS whereof the parties hereto have executed this lease as a deed on the date first hereinbefore written

8.14 It is always worthwhile checking to ensure that there is in fact no such agreement for lease which may need to be stamped. It can quite often be overlooked especially when there is a long period between exchange of agreements for lease and completion of the lease and it is worth remembering the circumstances in which it is necessary to pay stamp duty on the agreement for lease as opposed to the lease document itself. (See section 240 of the Finance Act 1994.)

8.15 Is the lease to be contracted out of the security of tenure provisions of the Landlord and Tenant Act 1954? If not, this clause should be deleted.

8.16 A break clause for the Tenant will have been agreed by negotiation. The first deletion shown is vital to ensure that the right to break is not lost. Compliance with the precondition attaching to the exercise of the break has been strictly interpreted by the courts; even a trivial breach of one of the more minor covenants would render the clause inoperative. The second amendment is self-explanatory. Why should only antecedent breaches by the tenant survive?

SCHEDULE 1 - THE PREMISES

The expression 'the Premises' includes those parts of the Building shown edged red on the Plan but excludes the roof and the roof space, the foundations, and all external, structural or loadbearing walls, columns, beams and supports (or as required in the circumstances)] including:

1. the paint paper and other decorative finishes applied to the interior of the external walls and columns of the Building but not any other part of the external walls and columns
2. the floor finishes but nothing below them
3. the ceiling finishes and any suspended ceilings but nothing above the ceiling finishes
4. any non-load-bearing internal walls wholly within the Premises
5. the inner half of the internal non-load-bearing walls dividing the Premises from other parts of the Building
6. the door and windows and the door and window frames
7. all additions and improvements
8. all fittings installed by the Landlord
9. all fixtures (whether or not fixed to the Premises at the commencement of the Term) except any installed by the Tenant that can be removed without defacing the Premises
10. any Conducting Media wholly in the Premises that exclusively serve the Premises

SCHEDULE 1 - THE PREMISES

When only part of a building is being leased, it is absolutely vital to clearly identify the extent of the building which comprises the premises since, most critically, the tenant's repairing obligation will only extend to the premises (as defined) as will all the other obligations of the tenant. Coupled with this, it is also vital for the tenant's adviser to look at the definition of the premises in conjunction with the definition of *Retained Parts* (see clause 1.36), since by virtue of clause 4.2.1 the landlord is obliged to use his best endeavours to provide the services and these include (in paragraph 2.11.1 of Schedule 6 (as amended)) the repair, replacement, renewal and decoration of the Retained Parts. What must be absolutely avoided is a situation where essential repairs which are not the tenant's responsibility are also not clearly the express obligation of the landlord since a situation could then arise where the responsibility for the repairs does not lie with either party. In *Adami v Lincoln Grange Management Ltd* [1998] 1 EGLR 58, the Court of Appeal held that no principle could be discerned which requires the implication on the part of a landlord to keep the structure of a building in good repair when the lease was silent on this point. While the maxim *contra proferentum* will apply against the person offering it (ie the landlord), it is not good practice to leave it to the courts to decide, most likely only after expensive litigation, where relative liabilities lie! The detailed definition of the premises should ensure that this does not happen. What is also absolutely imperative is that if a survey is undertaken (something the author strongly recommends *if* only for someone to have the opportunity to inspect the site and identify works that the tenant may require the landlord to carry out either as a precondition to taking the lease or with which to negotiate a rent-free period) and if there are any unusual features of the building the surveyor should be asked to give his view as to who should have the responsibility of repair and maintenance of these items.

In leases which comprise entire buildings, without any express provision to the contrary, both the sub-soil beneath and air space above would be included in the premises. These may be valuable assets or impose burdensome liabilities which both parties will need to consider.

SCHEDULE 2 - THE RIGHTS GRANTED

1 RIGHT TO USE THE COMMON PARTS

The right, subject to temporary interruption for repair, alteration, rebuilding or replacement, for the Tenant and all persons expressly or by implication authorised by him, in common with the Landlord and all other persons having a like right, to use appropriate areas of the Common Parts for all proper purposes in connection with the use and enjoyment of the Premises at such times as they are open in accordance with the Landlord's obligations in this Lease

2 PASSAGE AND RUNNING T other for any antecedent breachHROUGH THE ADJOINING CONDUITS

The right, subject to temporary interruption for repair, alteration or replacement, to the free passage and running of all services which now or at any time during the Term run through the appropriate Adjoining Conduits, in common with the Landlord and all other persons having a like right together with the right at reasonable times and on reasonable prior notice to have access to other parts of the Building for the purposes of maintenance and repair of the same

3 DISPLAY OF NAMEPLATES OR SIGNS

The right to have two nameplates or signs displayed in positions on the outside of the Building adjacent to its main entrance and in the reception area of the Building, of sizes to be specified by the Landlord (acting reasonably) showing the Tenant's name and any other details approved by the Landlord such approval not to be unreasonably withheld or delayed and PROVIDED ALWAYS that nothing in this paragraph or anywhere else in this lease shall preclude the Tenant from displaying its usual corporate or trade logo

4 RIGHT TO USE THE ADDITIONAL PARKING BAYS

4.1 The right to use the Additional Parking Bays or such other car parking bays as the Landlord from time to time reasonably designates in writing

5 SUPPORT

The rights of light air support protection shelter and all other easements and rights at the date of this Lease belonging to or enjoyed by the Premises

SCHEDULE 2 - THE RIGHTS GRANTED

2 – 1 The amendment here provides that any interruption in the right to use common parts is only a temporary interruption.

2 – 2 The first amendment achieves the same purpose as that referred to at paragraph 2 - 1 above. The second amendment ensures the tenant has the right to use any *services* which are installed at a future date, while the final amendment ensures that if it is necessary for whatever reason for the tenant to need to repair an Adjoining Conduit (eg landlord default) the necessary right exists to go into other parts of the building (including other areas constructed for letting) to carry out the repair and/or maintenance.

2 – 3 The first amendment once again introduces an element of reasonableness into the process of obtaining landlord's approval as to the specification for the signs etc. The second amendment (perhaps more importantly for the tenant) precludes the landlord from objecting to the tenant's usual trade insignia. The tenant's trade insignia is likely to be known to the landlord and this proviso enables the tenant to proceed without delay in exhibiting the nameplate or sign. (See clause 3.6.2.)

2 – 4 The amendment once again introduces the concept of reasonableness into the landlord's decision-making process.

2 – 5 (new) This amendment incorporates self-explanatory rights which are simply a reciprocation of those contained in paragraph 3 – 5 of Schedule 3.

6 EMERGENCY ACCESS

The right in the case of emergency of access through any adjoining or neighbouring parts of the Building

2 – 6 This right would be exercisable in the event of fire or any other emergency and is self-explanatory.

SCHEDULE 3 - THE RIGHTS RESERVED

All rights reserved in this Schedule are subject to the provisions of clause 4.4:

1 PASSAGE AND RUNNING THROUGH THE CONDUITS

1.1 The right to the free and uninterrupted passage and running of all appropriate services or supplies from and to other parts of the Building or any adjoining property of the Landlord in and through the Conduits and through any structures of a similar use or nature that may at any time be in over or under the Premises

2 CONSTRUCTION OF CONDUITS

2.1 ~~The right to construct and to maintain at any time any pipes, sewers, drains, mains, ducts, conduits, gutters, watercourses, wires, cables, laser optical fibres, data or impulse transmission, communication or reception systems, channels, flues and other necessary conducting media for the provision of services or supplies, including any fixings, louvres, cowls and any other ancillary apparatus for the benefit of any other part of the Building or any of the Adjoining Property~~

3 ACCESS

3.1 **Access to inspect**

3.1.1 The right at any time to enter, or in emergency to break into and enter, the Premises:

3.1.1.1 to inspect the condition and the state of repair of the Premises

3.1.1.2 to inspect, clean, connect with, repair, remove, replace with others, alter or execute any works whatever to or in connection with the conduits, easements, supplies or services referred to in paragraphs 3-1 and 3-2 where such viewing or work would not otherwise be reasonably practicable

3.1.1.3 to view the state and condition of and repair and maintain the Building where such viewing or work would not otherwise be reasonably practicable

3.1.1.4 to carry out work or do anything whatever that the Landlord is obliged to do under this Lease where such viewing or work would not otherwise be reasonably practicable

3.1.1.5 to take schedules or inventories of fixtures and other items to be yielded up at the end of the Term and

SCHEDULE 3 - THE RIGHTS RESERVED

The additional introductory wording, which is a qualification of all the rights reserved, ensures that the amendment which the tenant will hopefully have negotiated in clause 4.4 (new) applies in relation to the exercise of all rights reserved to the landlord which involve entry onto the premises. Such rights could be immensely disruptive to a tenant and a landlord would have difficulty in objecting to such a precondition.

3 – 2.1 This right, if included and then exercised by a landlord, could be hugely disruptive to a tenant and could make beneficial occupation by the tenant virtually untenable. It should be deleted in its entirety. Then, if the landlord wishes to undertake any of the works envisaged, some form of licence outside the scope of the lease would have to be negotiated.

3 – 3.1.1.2 The amendment ensures that, if it is reasonably practicable for the landlord to undertake the specified works without interrupting the tenant's occupation then the landlord should have no rights of access.

3 – 3.1.1.3 This amendment achieves the same purpose as the amendment to paragraph 3 – 3.1.1.2 above and seeks to ensure that if it is practicable for the landlord to exercise any of these rights without interrupting the tenant's beneficial occupation access will be denied.

3 – 3.1.1.4 See paragraphs 3 – 3.1.1.2 and 3 - 3.1.1.3 above.

3.1.1.6 to exercise any of the rights granted to the Landlord by this Lease

~~3.2~~ ~~**Access on renewal or rent review**~~

~~The right with the Surveyor and any person acting as the third party determining the Rent in default of agreement under the provisions for rent review contained in this Lease at any time to enter and to inspect and measure the Premises for all purposes connected with any pending or intended step under the 1954 Act or the implementation of the provisions for rent review~~

4 SCAFFOLDING

The right to erect scaffolding for any proper purpose connected with or related to the Building ~~even if it~~but only if the same does not restricts access to or the use and enjoyment of the Premises

5 SUPPORT

The rights of light, air, support, protection, shelter and all other easements and rights at the date of this Lease belonging to or enjoyed by other parts of the Building

6 RIGHT TO ERECT NEW BUILDINGS

6.1 Full right and liberty at any time after the date of this Lease:

6.1.1 to alter, raise the height of, or rebuild the Building, which expression here includes the Premises and

6.1.2 to erect any new buildings of any height on any adjoining property of the Landlord in such manner as the Landlord thinks fit even if they may obstruct, affect, or interfere with the amenity of or access to the Premises or the passage of light and air to the Premises, ~~and even~~but only if they do not affect the Premises or their use and enjoyment

3 – 3.2 This clause should be deleted in its entirety. The lease renewal or rent review procedures may place the parties in adversarial roles so that the tenant will not welcome such an opportunity for the landlord to cause disruption and potential embarrassment. In any event, paragraph 3 – 3.1.1.1 should contain the necessary rights for the landlord and should be sufficient for any legitimate inspection purpose. The landlord should have all the premises' dimensions and measurements available from the outset of the lease so that he is in a position to conduct the rent reviews as and when they occur. Having given up possession of the premises to the tenant for the contractual term granted by the lease the tenant should be entitled to rely on these arguments for deleting this clause.

3 - 4 The first amendment is self-explanatory, while the second amendment places a restriction on the exercise of the right so that the erection of scaffolding does not interfere with the tenant's use of the premises. There is absolutely no reason why the tenant should accept any scaffolding which interferes with his occupation which may, in any event, amount to a breach of the landlord's covenant for quiet enjoyment. If it does, then he should argue that there ought to be some sort of reduction in the rent together with payment of compensation while the obstruction subsists.

3 - 6.1.2 The same arguments apply here as those referred to in clause 3 - 4 above.

SCHEDULE 4 - THE RENT AND RENT REVIEW

1 DEFINITIONS

1.1 For all purposes of this schedule the terms defined in this paragraph 4-1 have the meanings specified

1.2 **'An arbitrator'**

References to 'an arbitrator' are references to a person appointed by agreement between the Landlord and the Tenant or, in the absence of agreement within 14 days of one of them giving notice to the other of his nomination, nominated by the President on the application of either made not earlier than 6 months before the relevant review date or at any time thereafter to determine the rent under this schedule

1.3 **'The Assumptions'**

'The Assumptions' means:

1.3.1 the assumption that no work has been carried out on the Premises during the Term by the Tenant, his subtenants or their predecessors in title that has diminished the rental value of the Premises other than work carried out in compliance with clause 3.7 STATUTORY OBLIGATIONS

1.3.2 the assumption that if the Premises have been destroyed or damaged they have been fully rebuilt or reinstated unless the failure to reinstate the Premises is due to any act or omission on behalf of the Landlord

1.3.3 the assumption that the covenants contained in this Lease on the part of ~~the Landlord and~~ the Tenant have been fully performed and observed

SCHEDULE 4 - THE RENT AND RENT REVIEW

While a detailed consideration of, arguably, the most important provisions in a commercial lease is beyond the scope of this book, certain core amendments should be sought by a tenant. It is important to establish early on in negotiations with the landlord or the landlord's representative what the purpose of the rent review clause is to be, if there is going to be one in the lease. The landlord will want to ensure that he obtains, at the very least, a return commensurate with market rents at the time the review takes place. On this basis, therefore, it is important, when representing the tenant, to ensure that this is exactly what the rent review clause achieves. The rent review clause is not designed to give the landlord any form of enhanced rental by way of a return over and above that which would be obtainable on a new letting at a market rent. From the tenant's point of view it is important, therefore, to ensure that there is never any question of a '*headline*' rental being obtained and that terms such as 'best' or 'highest' rent are also avoided when determining the open market rent. No doubt the tenant will also wish to avoid an upwards only rent review if he can negotiate this (see paragraph 4 – 2.1). A headline rent is probably best explained using an example. If a tenant agrees to take a lease for five years at a rental of £100,000 pa but he is also granted a twelve month rent-free period then, while the *headline* rent, ie the rent stated in the lease, remains at £100,000 pa, the *effective* rent payable is actually only £80,000 pa. This concept is vital in understanding the importance of certain disregards and assumptions because if the appropriate provisions are not deleted by the tenant's adviser and the lease is absolutely clear as to what is to be disregarded, ie any rent-free period, an effective rent of £80,000 pa would become an effective rent of £100,000 pa. It is vital therefore that all references to rent-free periods are carefully scrutinised in conjunction with the tenant's surveyor.

4 – 1.3.1 The words beginning '... other than ...' to the end of the paragraph should be included if they are not already there to ensure the tenant is not penalised by having had to pay for works which diminish the rental value only to have those works disregarded on review.

4 - 1.3.2 The addition here is designed to ensure that, if the premises are in a dilapidated state due to a fault on the part of the landlord and through no fault of the tenant, then any assumption about the hypothetical state of the premises reflects this. This may well result in a discount on the reviewed rent.

4 - 1.3.3 Landlords will often attempt to insert an assumption that his own covenants have been complied with. This is manifestly unfair on the tenant who may not be enjoying the full benefit of the premises due to some default on the part of the landlord. An assumption, therefore, that the landlord's covenants have been complied with should be resisted and the deletion achieves this. A landlord will argue that if at the date of review he is in breach he should not be saddled with a reduced rent until the next review date or the end of the term if that breach is soon to be remedied. Tenants should, in the face of that argument, argue

1.3.4 the assumption that the Premises are available to let by a willing landlord to a willing tenant in the open market by one lease ('the Hypothetical Lease') without a premium being paid by either party and with vacant possession

1.3.5 the assumption that the Premises have already been fitted out and equipped by and at the expense of the incoming tenant so that they are capable of being used by the incoming tenant from the beginning of the Hypothetical Lease for all purposes required by the incoming tenant that would be permitted under this Lease

1.3.6 the assumption that the Hypothetical Lease contains the same terms as this Lease except the amount of the Initial Rent and any rent-free period allowed to the Tenant for fitting out the Premises for his occupation and use at the commencement of the Term, but including the provisions for rent review on the Review Dates and except as set out in subparagraph 4-1.3.7

1.3.7 the assumption that the term of the Hypothetical Lease is equal in length to the <u>residue unexpired of the</u> Contractual Term and that such term begins on the relevant review date, that the rent commences to be payable on that date, and that the years during which the tenant covenants to decorate the Premises are at the same intervals after the beginning of the term of the Hypothetical Lease as those specified in this Lease

~~1.3.8 the assumption that the Hypothetical Lease will be renewed at the expiry of its term under the provisions of the 1954 Act and~~

~~1.3.9 the assumption that every prospective willing landlord and willing tenant is able to recover VAT in full~~

1.4 **'The Disregards'**

'The Disregards' means:

1.4.1 disregard of any effect on rent of the fact that the Tenant, his subtenants, or their predecessors in title or any lawful occupier have been in occupation of the Premises

1.4.2 disregard of any goodwill attached to the Premises because the business of the Tenant, his subtenants, or their predecessors in title in their respective businesses is or was carried on there and

1.4.3 disregard of any increase in rental value of the Premises attributable at the relevant review date to any improvement to the Premises carried out, ~~with consent where required~~, otherwise than in pursuance of an obligation except an obligation contained in clause 3.7 STATUTORY OBLIGATIONS to the Landlord or his predecessors in title either:

that there should be a provision whereby the arbitrator (or expert) fixing the reviewed rent in the absence of agreement is directed to establish two levels of rental; the first to subsist for so long as the breach itself subsists and the second to kick in once the breach complained of has been rectified.

4 – 1.3.5 Many tenants would argue that this assumption should be deleted in its entirety. If an actual tenant has already paid to fit out the Premises (with no initial rent-free period to compensate) it is never going to benefit from this expense if those works are always assumed to be there. It is the author's view, again trying to reflect reality as much as possible, that ideally the assumption should be deleted and the expert/arbitrator left to decide whether, at the time of review, a hypothetical tenant would get a rent-free period (and therefore a discount on the rent) for the cost of fitting out dependent on market conditions at the time of the review.

4 - 1.3.7 Reverting back to the argument set out above at the introduction to Schedule 4, it is important to try and draft the rent review clause to correspond as closely as possible to what actually exists, so that the contractual term of the hypothetical lease is equal to the unexpired residue of the contractual term at the actual date of review. If this has a depressing effect on rental values then so be it. An assumption on any other basis, ie for a term in excess of that which is, in fact, left departs from reality, is wholly artificial and, the author contends, unsustainable.

4 - 1.3.8 If there is a possibility that the *hypothetical lease* will be renewed then this is something no doubt the independent third party determining the rent will take into account when determining the review. He should not be directed to make an assumption like this, for example where the lease might be contracted out of the security of tenure provisions of the Landlord and Tenant Act 1954 or where it is known at the rent review date that the landlord is likely to have grounds for successfully opposing the grant of a new lease on the expiry of the term. The deletion reflects this.

4 - 1.3.9 This is a wholly false assumption and may well not in fact be the case. If it is the case then, as referred to above in paragraph 4 - 1.3.8, the arbitrator/expert will no doubt take account of it. If it is not then the review should reflect reality without false and distorting assumptions being introduced.

4 - 1.4.3 The deletion here meets the situation where an improvement may not have been formally authorised, eg where there was a *need* to carry out works and formal consent could not be obtained in time and that 'breach' was subsequently waived. The amendment will ensure that if works were, in fact, improvements then those works are not '*rentalised*' which means the reviewed rent will be uplifted to take account of that improvement. If the tenant has actually funded the improvement he will not thank his advisers if his rent is then subsequently enhanced by virtue of it.

1.4.3.1 by the Tenant, his subtenants, or their predecessors in title or any lawful occupier during the Term or during any period of occupation before the Term or

1.4.3.2 by any tenant or subtenant of the Premises or any lawful occupiers before the commencement of the Term provided that the Landlord or his predecessors in title have not since the improvement was carried out had vacant possession of the relevant part of the Premises and

~~1.4.3.3 disregard of the taxable status of the Landlord or the Tenant for the purpose of VAT~~

1.5 **'The President'**

1.5.1 'The President' means the President for the time being of the Royal Institution of Chartered Surveyors or any person authorised by him to make appointments on his behalf

1.6 **'A review period'**

1.6.1 References to 'a review period' are references to the period beginning on any review date and ending on the day before the next review date or in relation to the final review period the period beginning on the final review date and ending on the last day of the Contractual Term

2 ASCERTAINING THE RENT

2.1 The Rent

Until the First Review Date the Rent is to be the Initial Rent, and thereafter during each successive review period the Rent is to be a sum equal to ~~the greater of the rent payable under this Lease immediately before the relevant review date, or, if payment of rent has been suspended as provided for in this Lease, the rent that would have been payable had there been no such suspension, or~~ the revised rent ascertained in accordance with this schedule

2.2 Agreement of the Rent

Six months before each review date, time not being of the essence of the contract, the Landlord and the Tenant must ~~explore the possibility of reaching~~use reasonable endeavours to reach a written agreement as to the Rent for the following review period and the Rent for that period may be agreed at any time or, in the absence of agreement, is to be determined by an arbitrator not earlier than the relevant review date

2.3 Open market rent

The sum to be determined by an arbitrator must be the ~~best~~ sum at which he decides the Premises might reasonably be expected to be let in the open market at the relevant review date making the Assumptions but disregarding the Disregards

4 - 1.4.3.3 The same arguments apply here as those referred to in paragraphs 4 - 1.3.8 and 4 - 1.3.9 above. The review should take account of the actual status of the parties and not be based on assumptions that distort reality and, therefore, distort the open market rent that the tenant should, in fact, be paying.

4 - 1.6.1 As was seen in the amendment proposed to clause 3 - 1.3.7, the tenant would be ill-advised to allow a situation to arise whereby he faces a penultimate day rent review. The amendment at the end of this paragraph should be incorporated for the sake of consistency with the earlier amendment.

4 – 2.1 The deletion ensures that any rent review which takes place is not an upwards only rent review. At every rent review date the rent will therefore reflect a true open-market rent and again will not be distorted if rental values have fallen since the last rent review date. If the agreed heads of terms make it quite clear that any rent reviews are to be upwards only, it is vital to ensure that a tenant fully understands exactly what that means, ie the rent will *never* fall below the initial rent agreed at the start of the lease even if rental values fall drastically. The author contends that upwards only rent reviews are essentially unsustainable and if a landlord will not accept an upwards and downwards review (sometimes called an 'open market' review), a tenant's adviser should be arguing for a shorter term.

4 - 2.2 With respect, the author is not quite sure what the phrase '*...explore the possibility of reaching...*' means or is intended to achieve. The amendment uses words with which lawyers are familiar and which have been interpreted by the courts (see clause 5.6.3.1). Wording such as that used in this paragraph also avoids any '*time of the essence*' problems.

4 - 2.3 If there is no other amendment that the tenant can negotiate in the whole lease, this is the one he must stick out for. Inclusion of the word '*best*' means that if, when determining the rent, the expert or arbitrator considers that a range of possible awards is available to him, then, because of the use of the word '*best*' his award will be pitched at the highest figure and indeed any bid from a special bidder, eg a neighbour, will be taken into account. Unless there is a sustainable argument from the landlord (ie that the offices do represent the best offices available in the relevant market) then there is absolutely no reason why the word '*best*' should be included in the definition. The precedent here appoints the independent third party to act as an *arbitrator* here and not as an *expert.* While a detailed study of the differences is beyond the scope of this book, briefly, an expert is likely to be cheaper and quicker and usually less formal. An arbitrator has a statutory framework within which he must operate and has far greater powers. Indeed many see an arbitrator's view as a quasi-judicial one.

2.4 Conduct of the arbitration

The arbitration must be conducted in accordance with the Arbitration Act 1996, except that if the arbitrator dies or declines to act the President may, on the application of either the Landlord or the Tenant, appoint another in his place

2.5 Memoranda of agreement

Whenever the Rent has been ascertained in accordance with this schedule, memoranda to that effect must be signed by or on behalf of the Landlord and the Tenant and annexed to this document and its counterpart, and ~~the Tenant must pay both parties~~ each party is to pay its own costs in this respect

2.6 Reimbursement of costs

If, on publication of the arbitrator's award, the Landlord or the Tenant pays all his fees and expenses, the paying party may, in default of payment within 21 days of a demand to that effect, recover such proportion of them, if any, as the arbitrator awards against the other in the case of the Landlord as rent arrears or in the case of the Tenant by deduction from the Rent

3 PAYMENT OF THE RENT AS ASCERTAINED

3.1 Where the Rent is not ascertained by a review date

If the Rent payable during any review period has not been ascertained by the relevant review date, then rent is to continue to be payable at the rate previously payable, such payments being on account of the Rent for that review period

3.2 Where a review date is not a quarter day

If the Rent for any review period is ascertained on or before the relevant review date but that date is not a quarter day, then the Tenant must pay to the Landlord ~~on that review date~~ as soon as reasonably practicable after demand the difference between the Rent due for that quarter and the Rent already paid for it.

3.3 Back-payment where review delayed

If the Rent payable during any review period has not been ascertained by the relevant review date, then the Tenant must pay to the Landlord ~~on~~as soon as reasonably practicable after the date on which the Rent is agreed or the arbitrator's award is received by him, any shortfall between the Rent that would have been paid for that period had it been ascertained on or before the relevant review date and the payments made by the Tenant on account and any VAT payable thereon~~, and interest, at the Interest Rate in respect of each~~

4 - 2.5 There is no reason and, in the author's view, no sustainable argument why the tenant should pay the costs of the landlord for recording the result of either an agreed or a disputed award.

4 - 3.2 This amendment gives the tenant a period of grace within which to pay any uplift in the rental. It may be that a substantial hike could cause real cash flow difficulties for the tenant if the shortfall fell to be payable immediately. The landlord has the ultimate sanction of suing the tenant to enforce the award.

4 - 3.3 The first amendment seeks to achieve the same effect as that referred to in clause 4 - 3.2 above. The subsequent deletion deprives the landlord of any incentive to delay resolution of the review so that any shortfall is subject to an interest payment for the longest possible period and giving a possibly unfair return to the landlord. The landlord may argue that a properly-advised tenant will have been told by his adviser what the likely outcome of the review will be and should, therefore, have made contingency plans by placing the amount of any difference in an interest-bearing account to mitigate the harshness of any interest penalty. The

~~instalment of rent due on or after that review date on the amount by which the instalment of the Rent that would have been paid had it been ascertained exceeds the amount paid by the Tenant on account, the interest to be payable for the period from the date on which the instalment was due up to the date of payment of the shortfall~~

3.4 Effect of counter-inflation provisions

If at any review date a statute prevents, restricts or modifies the Landlord's right either to review the Rent in accordance with this Lease or to recover any increase in the Rent, then the Landlord may, when the restriction or modification is removed, relaxed or varied during the Contractual Term without prejudice to his rights, if any, to recover any rent the payment of which has only been deferred by statute—on giving not less than 1 ~~week~~month nor more than 3 ~~week~~month's notice to the Tenant at any time within 6 months of the restriction or modification being removed, relaxed or varied, time being of the essence, require the Tenant to proceed with any review of the Rent that has been prevented or to review the Rent further where the Landlord's right was restricted or modified. The date of expiry of the notice is to be treated as a review date—provided that nothing in this paragraph is to be construed as varying any subsequent review date. The Landlord may recover any increase in the Rent with effect from the earliest date permitted by law

compromise usually agreed is that interest should be payable at the *base rate* of a particular financial institution rather than the penal rate referred to in clause 1.20.

4 - 3.4 The first amendment ensures that there can be no retrospective ground arguable to the landlord once the contractual term of the lease has ended to pursue the tenant for rent. The second and third amendments provide for the tenant being given reasonable time within which to gear up for the impending review.

SCHEDULE 5 - THE OFFICE COVENANTS

1 USE

1.1 Use as offices

The Tenant must not use the Premises for any purpose other than as offices connected with its business of [ ]

1.2 Permitted hours

Without prior notification ~~T~~the Tenant must not use and occupy the Premises ~~during~~outside the Permitted Hours ~~only~~

1.3 Cesser of business

The Tenant must not cease carrying on business in the Premises or leave the Premises continuously unoccupied for more than 1 month without notifying the Landlord of his intention so to do

1.4 Noxious discharges

The Tenant must not knowingly discharge into any of the Conduits or the Adjoining Conduits any oil, grease or other deleterious matter, or any substance that ~~might~~is likely to be or become a source of danger or injury to the drainage system

SCHEDULE 5 - THE OFFICE COVENANTS

5 - 1.1 The proposed amendment is drafted so that the permitted user is as narrowly defined as possible while consistent with the tenant's current proposals and his projected plans for his business. The primary reason for this is to ensure that, at review, the narrowly defined use has the greatest possible effect in reducing or keeping down the rental value. This is unlikely to prove to be acceptable to the landlord but should be sought nonetheless. From a practical point of view it is important to ensure that while being as narrowly defined as possible is ideal for the purpose of the rent review, the user clause must be wide enough to ensure the tenant can expand his business as he chooses and wide enough to ensure that should the tenant ever wish to dispose of the lease it is as marketable as possible. Too narrow a clause may mean the tenant could only dispose of the lease to a competitor. The circumstances of each particular letting may dictate where the greatest emphasis lies. If the permitted use for the premises has been defined by reference to the Use Classes Order it is important to ensure that if a particular Use Classes Order is referred to complications do not arise with its interpretation as a result of clause 1.46.5. The author would suggest that if the permitted use is defined by reference to the Use Classes Order then the following words be added, '...*in relation to which the provisions of clause 1.46.5 shall not apply* ...'.

5 - 1.2 The purpose of this amendment is simply to ensure that, if the tenant requires it, 24-hour access to the property is available. There are not many businesses nowadays which can restrict themselves to working only during certain defined hours. If clause 1.30 has been successfully deleted this paragraph can be deleted in its entirety. In addition, if the premises are retail premises, account must be taken of the Sunday Trading Act 1994.

5 - 1.3 There may be good commercial or operational reasons why the premises are to be vacated, eg following a corporate restructuring it may be that the functions previously performed at these offices have been relocated and they have no further use. An absolute obligation to remain in occupation in the premises might well be against the strategic aims of the tenant who might have to live with a long period of vacancy should the lease be difficult to assign. The problems that tenants of retail premises have run into over '*keep open*' covenants should be a warning to all tenants of the danger of the landlord bringing a claim for damages for breach of this provision.

5 - 1.4 The first amendment imparts knowledge to negate strict liability (see clause 3.15.1) and the second imposes a greater burden of proof.

1.5 **Window cleaning**

The Tenant must clean both sides of all windows and window frames in the Premises ~~at least once every month~~as often as occasion shall reasonably require

1.6 **Sound audible outside**

The Tenant must not play or use in the Premises any musical instrument, audio or other equipment or apparatus that produces sound that may be heard outside the Premises

1.7 **Ceiling and floor loading**

1.7.1 **Heavy items**

The Tenant must not bring onto or permit to remain on the Premises any safes, machinery, goods or other articles that will ~~or may~~ strain or damage the Premises or any part of them

1.7.2 **Protection of ceilings**

The Tenant must not without the consent of the Landlord (such consent not to be unreasonably withheld or delayed) suspend anything from any ceiling on the Premises

1.8 **Expert advice**

If the Tenant applies for the Landlord's consent under paragraph 1.7.2 the Landlord may consult any engineer or other person in relation to the ceiling loading proposed by the Tenant, and the Tenant must repay the reasonable and proper fees of the engineer or other person to the Landlord as soon as reasonably practicable following~~on~~ demand

2 **COMMON PARTS**

2.1 **Care of the Common Parts**

The Tenant must not cause the Common Parts or any other land, roads or pavements adjoining the Building and belonging to the Landlord to become untidy or dirty

2.2 **Display of goods outside**

The Tenant must not display or deposit anything whatsoever outside the Premises for display or sale or for any other purpose, or save in emergency cause any obstruction of the Common Parts

5 - 1.5 While the amendment speaks for itself, it is important to bear in mind the wider implications of very strictly drawn clauses and the inter-relationship they have with other clauses in the lease, eg a tenant's break clause which is conditional upon *strict compliance* with covenants elsewhere (see clause 8.16). In the light of the interpretation placed by the court on such strict preconditions even an immaterial breach (such as default in window cleaning) could prove fatal from the tenant's point of view and so result in the loss of a very precious commodity such as a break clause.

5 - 1.7.1 The clause as originally drafted gives the landlord an arguable case that the tenant's proposals may cause the strain or damage without any form of quantitative assessment. The deletion prevents this happening.

5 - 1.7.2 The proposed amendment changes an absolute prohibition into a qualified one and gives the tenant the opportunity to argue that the landlord is acting unreasonably.

5 - 1.8 The amendments here are self-explanatory.

5 - 2.1 It is unfair that the landlord should seek to police areas outside its own ownership by imposing restrictions on the tenant and the amendment meets this point

5 - 2.2 The amendment here is self-explanatory and would allow the tenant to obstruct the common part in the case of an emergency.

2.3 **Machinery**

2.3.1 **Noisy machinery**

The Tenant must not <u>without the Landlord's consent (such consent not to be unreasonably withheld or delayed)</u> install or use in or on the Premises any machinery or apparatus that will cause noise or vibration that can be heard or felt in nearby premises or outside the Premises or that may cause structural damage

2.3.2 **Maintenance of machinery**

In order to avoid <u>physical</u> damage to the Premises, the Tenant must keep all machinery and equipment on the Premises ('the Machinery') properly maintained and in good working order and for that purpose must employ reputable contractors ~~to be approved by the Landlord whose approval may not be unreasonably refused~~ ('the Contractors') to carry out <u>as often as occasion shall reasonably require</u> ~~regular periodic~~ inspection and maintenance of the Machinery

2.4 **Renewal of parts**

The Tenant must renew all working and other parts of the Machinery as and when <u>reasonably</u> necessary or when recommended by the Contractors

~~2.5~~ ~~**Operation**~~

~~The Tenant must ensure by directions to his staff and otherwise that the Machinery is properly operated~~

3 UNLOADING

3.1 **Loading bays to be used**

The Tenant must not load or unload any goods or materials from any vehicle unless the vehicle is parked in the loading bay coloured yellow on ~~the~~ Plan <u>No. 3</u>, and must not cause congestion of that or any adjoining loading bays or <u>unnecessary</u> inconvenience to any other user of it or them

3.2 **Standing vehicles**

The Tenant must not permit any vehicles belonging to him or any persons calling on the Premises expressly or by implication with his authority to stand on the service roads or any pavements or, except when and for so long as they are actually loading or unloading goods and materials, on the loading bays, and must use ~~his best~~<u>reasonable</u> endeavours to ensure that such persons do not permit any vehicle so to stand

5 - 2.3.1 The amendment provides that every application by the tenant to install machinery or apparatus is considered on its own merits. It may well be that the criteria referred to do, in fact, provide the benchmark against which the landlord will be able to judge whether he has grounds for withholding consent but at least, once again, the amendment inserts the concept of reasonableness and gives the tenant the opportunity of arguing the point.

5 - 2.3.2 These are, the author contends, matters which are the personal responsibility of the tenant in running his business and have nothing whatsoever to do with the landlord. The word *reputable* gives the landlord the necessary comfort.

5 - 2.4 This amendment is self-explanatory.

5 - 2.5 This again is an internal management issue for the tenant and has no relevance to the relationship of landlord and tenant. The clause should be deleted on this basis.

5 - 3.1 The first amendment seeks to ensure, once again, consistency in referring to the plans. The second reflects the fact that unloading a vehicle, even in designated parking areas, will inevitably on occasions cause an inconvenience to somebody or other.

5 - 3.2 The amendment here is made in consequence of the court's decisions that *best endeavours* is something more onerous than *reasonable endeavours* (see clause 5.6.3.1) and, in the context of what is envisaged, an obligation to use best endeavours may involve expenditure of money or the involvement of management time on the tenant's part wholly out of proportion to their ability to control visitors to the premises.

3.3 **Use of goods entrances required**

The Tenant must not convey any goods or materials to or from the Premises except through the entrances and service areas provided for the purpose

4 **HEATING, COOLING AND VENTILATION**

4.1 **Interference prohibited**

The Tenant must not knowingly do anything that interferes with the heating, cooling ventilation or air conditioning of the Common Parts or that imposes an additional load on any heating, cooling ventilation or air conditioning plant and equipment in the Building

4.2 **Operation of equipment**

During the Permitted Hours, the Tenant must operate the ventilation equipment in the Premises in accordance with the reasonable written regulations made by the Landlord from time to time for that purpose and served on the Tenant

5 **REGULATIONS**

5.1 The tenant must comply with all written regulations made in the interests of good estate management by the Landlord from time to time for the management of the Building PROVIDED ALWAYS that if there shall be any inconsistency between any such regulations and the terms of this lease then the terms of this lease shall prevail

6 **NAMEPLATES OR SIGNS**

6.1 Before or as soon as reasonably practicable after occupying the Premises for the purpose of his business at the commencement of the Term and following a permitted assignment or subletting, the Tenant must provide the Landlord with details of the information that he wishes to have included in the nameplates or signs referred to in paragraph 2-3 DISPLAY OF NAME-PLATES OR SIGNS, and must pay to the Landlord as soon as reasonably practicable following~~on~~ demand the reasonable and proper charges of the Landlord for making and installing every such nameplate or sign

5 - 4.1 The amendment is self-explanatory and once again avoids the harsh consequences of strict liability.

5 - 4.2 The first amendment provides that any such regulations which are needed must be both reasonable and have been committed to paper so there is no dispute as to their content. The second amendment prevents the tenant being liable where written regulations may have been made but he has not had notice of these.

5 - 5.1 The author's first instinct is to delete this clause in its entirety. The lease has been *freely* negotiated between the parties and therefore *any* provision which seeks to give either party the right to unilaterally alter the basis on which the landlord manages the building or otherwise must be manifestly unfair. However, this is likely to be resisted by a landlord and therefore the first two amendments ensure that any such regulations arise in the interests of good estate management and are not simply introduced to alter, unilaterally, the arrangements for management of the building or otherwise agreed in the lease negotiations. The proviso ensures that any such regulations will not prevail of they are inconsistent with the terms of the lease so, in effect, the landlord can add new regulations but *not* alter existing contractual obligations.

5 - 6. Ideally the tenant should seek to strike this clause out in its entirety. If not successful then the tenant should attempt to incorporate those amendments indicated all of which are self-explanatory. To have an *absolute* obligation to provide this information - and indeed to have such an obligation at all - may be contrary to the tenant's policy; for good commercial reasons such as their wish to keep his presence within a particular building a secret for as long as possible.

SCHEDULE 6 - THE SERVICE CHARGE AND SERVICES

1 DEFINITIONS

In this schedule the terms defined below have the meanings given in this paragraph

1.1 **'A financial year'**

References to 'a financial year' are references to the period commencing on 1 January in any year and ending on 31 December in the same year or such other annual period as the Landlord in his reasonable discretion determines as being that for which his accounts, either generally or in respect of the Building, are to be made up

1.2 **'The Management Premises'**

'The Management Premises' means all if any of the administrative and control offices and storage areas, staff rooms and other areas properly maintained by the Landlord for the purpose of managing the Building and performing the Landlord's obligations under this Lease together with any living accommodation provided by the Landlord for security guards, caretakers or other staff employed by him for purposes connected with the Building

1.3 **'Other lettable premises'**

References to 'other lettable premises' are references to premises in the Building that are let, or are from time to time allocated for designed for letting, by the Landlord, other than the Premises, and respectively include and exclude, where applicable, the equivalent parts of the Building included in and excluded from the Premises as described in Schedule 1 THE PREMISES

1.4 **'The Plant'**

'The Plant' means all the electrical, mechanical and other plant, machinery, equipment, furnishings, furniture, fixtures and fittings of ornament or utility in use for common benefit from time to time on, in or at the Building, including, without prejudice to the generality of the foregoing, goods and passenger lifts, lift shafts, escalators, passenger conveyors, heating, cooling, lighting ventilation and air conditioning equipment, cleaning equipment, internal and public telephones, public address systems, fire precaution equipment, fire and burglar alarm systems, closed circuit television, refuse compactors and all other such equipment, including stand-by and emergency systems

SCHEDULE 6 - THE SERVICE CHARGE AND SERVICES

6 - 1.1 The first amendment seeks to ensure that the landlord does not manipulate the accounting reference dates each year to his own ends. The second amendment qualifies the otherwise unfettered discretion of the landlord in the operation of his wider accounting procedures.

6 - 1.2 The clause, as originally drafted, is far too wide from the tenant's point of view and, the author contends, absolutely unacceptable. If the landlord considers it necessary to provide living accommodation for security guards, caretakers or other staff employed by him for management reasons this is not something which the tenants in the building should actually pay for. To sustain an argument for including the deleted words, the landlord would have to show a very high degree of benefit to the tenant and other occupiers of the building.

6 - 1.3 It may appear here that the amendment does not add anything to the wording as originally drafted but the author would contend that this gives a narrower construction and is, therefore, preferable.

2 SERVICE CHARGE PROVISIONS

2.1 Certificate of the Landlord's Expenses

As soon as reasonably practicable after (but in any event within 2 months of the end of) each financial year the Landlord must ensure that the Accountant issues a certificate addressed to the Tenant containing a full and accurate summary of the Landlord's Expenses for that financial year, and a full and accurate summary of any expenditure that formed part of the Landlord's Expenses in respect of a previous financial year but has not been taken into account in the certificate for any previous financial year. ~~A copy of the certificate must be supplied by the Landlord to the Tenant~~In this Certificate the Accountant is to acknowledge that he has a duty of care to the Tenant

2.2 Omissions from the certificate

Omission by the Accountant from a certificate of the Landlord's Expenses of any expenditure incurred in the financial year to which the certificate relates is ~~not~~ to preclude the inclusion of that expenditure in any subsequent certificate

2.3 Deemed Landlord's Expenses

In any financial year the Landlord's Expenses are to be deemed to include:

2.3.1 such fair and reasonable part of all costs and expenditure in respect of or incidental to all or any of the recurring services and other matters referred to in paragraph 6-3, whenever paid or incurred ~~whether before or~~ (Provided the same are incurred during the Term) ~~including reasonable provision for anticipated expenditure as the Surveyor in his discretion allocates to that financial year~~ and

~~2.3.2~~ ~~an amount equal to the fair annual rental value of the Management Premises, as certified by the Surveyor and if the Landlord or a person connected with the Landlord or employed by the Landlord attends to (1) the supervision and management of the provision of services for the Building, and/or (2) the preparation of statements or certificates of the Landlord's Expenses, and/or (3) the auditing of the Landlord's Expenses, and/or (4) the collection of rents from the Building, then an expense is to be deemed to be paid or a cost incurred by the Landlord, being a fee not exceeding that which independent agents might properly have charged for the same work~~

2.4 Certificates conclusive

Any certificate of the Landlord's Expenses, and any certificate of the Surveyor or Accountant in connection with the Landlord's Expenses, is (save in relation to manifest error or fraud) to be conclusive as to the matters it purports to certify

6 - 2.1 The first amendment imposes a strict time limit within which the landlord's certificate as to the service charge expenditure must be issued to the tenant. In the author's experience many landlords are often guilty of serious delay in providing an accurate or detailed summary of the service charge expenditure but, unfortunately, many tenants are just as bad in chasing them up! The second and third amendments attempt to ensure that the landlord does not give a 'back of the fag packet' summary by putting him under an obligation to prepare a full and accurate summary of the service charge expenditure. The final amendment to this paragraph will leave the accountant in no doubt that he is liable to be sued by the tenant if he is negligent, breaching the duty of care he owes to the tenant. While this will not prove attractive to either the landlord or the accountant, it is certainly something that the tenant should press for. The tenant should argue that it is, after all, *his* money (and that of his co-tenants in the building) which the summary and the certificate relate to.

6 - 2.2 This amendment provides that if through bad or inadequate accounting or management practices an item of expenditure is overlooked in any year there is no reason why subsequently the tenant should be liable to pay for this oversight. While this argument is not likely to find favour with the landlord because he will argue that the services have been provided to the benefit of the tenant, it will ensure accurate accountability on a year-on-year basis.

6 - 2.3.1 The first amendment, once again, will ensure that all the recovery of expenditure under the service charge is dealt with on a year-on-year basis. There is no reason why a current tenant in occupation should subsidise a former tenant by contributing to an item of service charge expenditure incurred before he himself took up occupation and from which he derived no benefit. Taking the line of the landlord's drafting to the extreme, this would mean that all items of capital expenditure incurred in relation to provision of services could be recharged to the tenants subsequently rather than, as they clearly should do, form part of the landlord or developer's development or initial fit out costs; this, clearly, is unreasonable and unacceptable from the tenant's point of view. The final deletion relating to '*anticipated expenditure*' may be more difficult to sustain but inclusion of the word '*reasonable*' to qualify the anticipated expenditure may prove to be an acceptable compromise.

6 - 2.3.2 The author finds this clause unacceptable in its entirety. It should be strongly resisted and deleted. The only elements which could prove to be acceptable as a compromise are those dealing with the management functions which the landlord provides 'in-house' as opposed to those subsidising of the nominal rental for the management premises.

6 - 2.4 This amendment is self-explanatory and provides the tenant with a peg on which to hang an argument if either of these two eventualities exist.

2.5 **Payment**

Subject to any maximum payment agreed elsewhere in the Schedule for each financial year the Tenant must pay the Service Charge Percentage of the Landlord's Expenses

2.6 **Variation of the Service Charge Percentage**

The Service Charge Percentage may be varied to the extent that the Surveyor (acting reasonably) considers appropriate

2.7 **Landlord's contribution**

The Landlord is to have no liability to contribute to the Landlord's Expenses except in relation to any other lettable premises for which no contribution is payable by an occupier or other person

2.8 **Payment on account**

For each financial year the Tenant must pay to the Landlord on account of the Service Charge such a sum as the Surveyor (acting reasonably) certifies to be fair and reasonable having regard to the likely amount of the Service Charge up to a maximum of £[ ] for any one financial year. That sum must be paid in advance, ~~without deduction or set off,~~ by equal instalments on the usual quarter days, the first instalment to be paid on the quarter day immediately before the commencement of the financial year in question and is to be held by the Landlord in a separate nominated account (interest accruing to the amount) until such money is actually expended by the Landlord, the Tenant being given credit for any interest so accruing. If in all the circumstances he deems it fair and reasonably to do so then ~~D~~during any financial year the Surveyor may revise the contribution on account of the Service Charge for that financial year so as to take into account any actual or expected increase in expenditure, and as soon as reasonably practicable after a revision the Surveyor must certify the amount of the revised contribution

2.9 **Service charge for the first financial year**

The sum payable for the financial year current at the date of this document is to be the Initial Provisional Service Charge, of which the Tenant must, on the date of this document, pay to the Landlord a due proportion calculated from day to day in respect of the period from the date hereof to the next quarter day after the date of this document

2.10 **Final account and adjustments**

As soon as reasonably practicable (but in any event within 2 months) after the end of each financial year, the Landlord must furnish to the Tenant with an account of the Service Charge payable by him for that financial year, credit being given for payments made by the Tenant on account. ~~Within 7 days of~~As soon as reasonably practicable after

6 - 2.6 This amendment is self-explanatory and again introduces the concept of reasonableness.

6 - 2.8 What a tenant ideally wants at the outset is, as accurately as possible, an estimate of his total expenditure in respect of the premises for at least the first three or five years of the lease depending on the frequency of the rent review dates. A service charge provision makes such an accurate estimate almost, if not actually, impossible bearing in mind its fluctuating nature. While, no doubt, the tenant will have made enquiries, either prior to the grant of the lease or prior to the assignment, as to whether or not in the foreseeable future any major capital expenditure on the premises is known or anticipated it is not always possible for the landlord to predict them or he may not choose to show his hand. One way to ensure that there is a fixed liability is to *cap* a service charge such that it never exceeds an annual figure either expressed to be a certain amount of expenditure per square foot or a global figure for each year possibly increased annually either by reference to a fixed percentage or by reference to increases in the retail price index. This amendment ensures that this idea is at least considered. Many landlords seek to resist a cap on the basis that they want clean leases and do not want to have to subsidise management expenses from their rental income. Whether this proves to be acceptable is likely to be dependent on the relative bargaining positions of the parties. It is something which should however be considered. The deletion has been fully discussed at clause 3.11 while the additional reference to payment into a separate account is self-explanatory. The final amendment qualifies the ability of the surveyor to review the percentage contribution so that it must be fair and reasonable in all the circumstances for this to happen.

6 - 2.10 The first amendment is the same amendment as that made to clause 6 - 2.1 with the same arguments applying for its inclusion. The second amendment seeks to ensure that a hefty service charge balance does not place the tenant in cash-flow difficulties, while the final amendment provides for repayment of any credit balance on the service charge account at the end of the term when the tenant vacates. It is the author's

the furnishing of such an account, the Tenant must pay the Service Charge, or any balance of it payable, to the Landlord. The Landlord must allow any amount overpaid by the Tenant to him against future payments of Service Charge, whether on account or not~~.~~ And at the end of the Term the Landlord must repay any overpayment forthwith.

2.11 **The Services**

The Services are:

2.11.1 repairing and, whenever ~~the Landlord regards it as necessary in order to repair,~~ incapable of economic repair replacing or renewing and decorating the Retained Parts

2.11.2 operating, maintaining, repairing and, whenever ~~the Landlord, considers it appropriate,~~ incapable of economic repair renewing, replacing or modifying the Plant

2.11.3 placing and running maintenance contracts for the Building,

2.11.4 providing the Plant that the Landlord~~,~~ acting reasonably considers necessary or desirable, or that is required by law or by any government department or local, public or regulatory or other authority or court to be supplied and maintained, (but excluding ~~including~~ the initial capital expenditure) and including expenditure on replacement of any machinery (including motor vehicles) articles and materials for, for example, refuse collection and fire fighting,

2.11.5 providing suitable facilities for disposing of refuse, compacting it or removing it from the Building

2.11.6 supplying hot and cold water to the lavatory facilities in the Retained Parts during normal business hours, and providing towels, soap, toilet paper and other appropriate supplies, and staffing the lavatory facilities

2.11.7 providing lighting in the Retained Parts

2.11.8 providing central heating and if appropriate air conditioning to the Premises and the Common Parts during the Permitted Hours

2.11.9 cleaning the windows and other glass of the Retained Parts

2.11.10 supplying, maintaining, servicing and keeping in good condition and, wherever incapable of economic repair ~~the Landlord considers it appropriate,~~ renewing and replacing all fixtures, fittings, furnishings, equipment and any other things the Landlord ~~may~~acting reasonably considers desirable for performing the Services or for the appearance or upkeep of the Retained Parts

2.11.11 carrying out inspections and tests of the Retained Parts, including the Plant, that the Landlord acting reasonably from time to time considers necessary or desirable

experience that in such circumstances landlords may well try to ensure that there is little if any refund due to the tenant and this matter needs to be closely watched by the tenant in questioning the landlord's financial management.

6 - 2.11.1 There is a fundamental issue to be addressed here in relation to the service charge provision as a whole. This is whether or not the tenant is prepared to accept that in addition to his obligations to contribute to maintenance and repair, the service charge provision should go beyond this (with financial implications for the tenant) and extend to replacing or renewing any items to which the service charge relates which the landlord may want to improve or repair. If the principle for such replacement or renewal is acceptable to the tenant the amendment here seeks to ensure that the obligation to replace and renew (which is likely to prove more costly than simply maintaining and repairing) will only apply when the possibilities for repair have been exhausted. The same principle does, of course, apply to the tenant's repair obligations generally. (See clause 3.4.1.)

6 - 2.11.2 The same arguments can be put forward here as in relation to clause 6 - 2.11.1.

6 - 2.11.4 Again it is necessary to decide whether as a point of principle the service charge is to cover these items. If so, the amendments seek to limit the circumstances in which the provisions would apply so that the landlord is not given a free hand. It is the author's view that the provision of many of the items referred to is a management or investment expense for which the landlord should be responsible and not, therefore, a cost which should be passed on through the service charge and be payable by the tenant.

6 - 2.11.8 Once again, this is a matter of principle. Should the tenant be funding air-conditioning as it will no doubt improve the capital value of the premises? The installation of air-conditioning in the premises and common parts once its initial construction has been completed is likely to prove so troublesome and inconvenient that many tenants will want to resist this.

6 - 2.11.10 Once again the same arguments has to be considered here as in relation to clause 6 - 2.11.1.

6 - 2.11.11 This amendment is self-explanatory.

2.11.12 planting, tidying, tending and landscaping any appropriate part of the Common Parts in such manner as the Landlord <u>acting reasonably</u> from time to time considers appropriate

2.11.13 providing, replacing and renewing trees, shrubs, flowers, grass and other plants, flags, decorative lights and other decorations, decorative or drinking fountains or other amenities that the Landlord <u>acting reasonably</u> from time to time thinks fit to provide or maintain in the Building, and providing~~,~~<u> and</u> maintaining, ~~replacing and renewing~~ seats or benches in the Common Parts

2.11.14 employing such persons as the Landlord~~,~~<u> acting reasonably</u> considers necessary or desirable <u>in the interests of good estate management</u> from time to time in connection with providing any of the Services, performing the Landlord's other obligations in this Lease ~~and collecting rents accruing to the Landlord from the Building, with all incidental expenditure including, but without limiting the generality of the above, remuneration, payment of statutory contributions and such other health, pension, welfare, redundancy and similar or ancillary payments and any other payments the Landlord thinks desirable or necessary, and providing work clothing~~

~~2.11.15 discharging any amounts the Landlord may be liable to pay towards the expense of making, repairing, maintaining, rebuilding and cleaning anything—for example ways, roads, pavements, sewers, drains, pipes, watercourses, party walls, party structures, party fences and other conveniences—that are appurtenant to the Building or are used for the Building in common with any adjoining property of the Landlord~~

2.11.16 erecting, providing, maintaining, <u>and when incapable of economic repair</u> renewing and replacing notice boards, notices and other signs in the Building as the Landlord, <u>acting reasonably,</u> from time to time considers appropriate

~~2.11.17 administering and managing the Building, performing the Services, performing the Landlord's other obligations in this Lease and preparing statements or certificates of and auditing the Landlord's Expenses,~~

2.11.18 providing and performing all services of any kind whatsoever that the Landlord, acting reasonably<u> and in the interests of good estate management and for the benefit of the tenants in the Building</u>, from time to time provides

2.11.19 discharging all existing or future taxes, rates, charges, duties, assessments, impositions and outgoings whatsoever in respect of the Retained Parts, including, without prejudice to the generality of the above, those for water, electricity, gas and telecommunications

6 - 2.11.12 This amendment is self-explanatory.

6 - 2.11.13 The first amendment is self-explanatory while the second is based on the *replacing and renewing* argument referred to in 6 – 2.11.1. It is the author's view that replacing and renewing seats or benches in the common parts goes beyond what is envisaged by traditional service charge provisions and should be deleted. If not, where will it all end? What benefit does this bring to the tenant? This example does highlight the need for the tenant to consider carefully each element of all the service charge provisions on their own merits and question their appropriateness in relation to the premises and building to which the provisions relate.

6 - 2.11.14 The first two amendments are self-explanatory. To charge a tenant for collecting the rents which he has to pay is surely rubbing salt into his wounds and should be resisted. The other items deleted in this clause are, once again, items so far removed from providing services for the tenant in his enjoyment of the premises that they themselves again ought to be deleted.

6 - 2.11.15 An obligation to contribute towards the items referred to in this clause as originally drawn is no doubt a matter the landlord will have taken on board in deciding whether or not to purchase the freehold or the head leasehold interest in the building. These are matters which relate to the freehold and not to the tenant's occupation of the premises. If there is a potential liability on the part of the landlord here then this should have been taken into account in the rental negotiations.

6 - 2.11.16 The first amendment is based on the same arguments as are referred to in paragraph 6 - 2.11.1. The second amendment provides that the concept of reasonableness on the part of the landlord is introduced in deciding whether or not it needs to undertake such matters.

6 - 2.11.17 This clause as originally drawn again rubs salt into the tenant's wounds. If the landlord wishes to farm out management of the building then this is a *pure* management cost which he himself should absorb. This argument is unlikely to find much favour with the landlord who will almost certainly want to pass on such costs to all the tenants of the building. If the clause cannot be negotiated out then at least some fetter on what the landlord can charge should be inserted, eg a *reasonable and proper* sum or an agreed fixed sum or a percentage of the overall service charge.

6 - 2.11.18 If additional services other than those specifically set out are to be provided by virtue of this *sweeper clause* there must be some benefit in it for the tenant or the majority of the tenants in the building. The landlord should not be able to implement a scheme within the building to make unlet premises more attractive for the purpose of securing a new letting .

2.11.20 policing the Building, controlling traffic and pedestrians and providing such security staff as the Landlord acting reasonably from time to time thinks fit and proper, and providing, maintaining, ~~replacing and renewing~~ security equipment in the Building

~~2.11.21 paying any interest on any loan or overdraft raised for the purpose of defraying the Landlord's Expenses~~

~~2.11.22 taking any steps the Landlord, acting reasonably, from time to time considers appropriate for complying with, making representations against, or otherwise contesting or dealing with any statutory or other obligation affecting or alleged to affect the Building, including any notice, regulation or order of any government department, local, public, regulatory or other authority or court, compliance with which is not the direct liability of the Tenant or any Tenant of any part of the Building~~

2.11.23 discharging the cost of any service or matter the Landlord thinks proper for the better and more efficient management and use of the Building and the comfort and convenience of its occupants

~~2.11.24 renting any item used for carrying out any of the matters referred to in this schedule~~

2.11.25 abating any legal nuisance affecting the Building, except to the extent that abating it is the liability of any tenant of the Building and

2.11.26 keeping appropriate areas of the Common Parts open for servicing the Premises and other units in the Building from time to time

6 - 2.11.20 The first amendment is self-explanatory and the second amendment reflects the principle discussed at paragraph 6 - 2.11.1 above.

6 - 2.11.21 If the landlord cannot fund items of expenditure such as these then it is completely iniquitous that the tenant should pay the interest costs incurred on money borrowed to provide them. This clause is absolutely unacceptable from a tenant's point of view and should be deleted.

6 - 2.11.22 The same arguments which were put forward in relation to paragraph 6 - 2.11.15 apply here also. These are *pure* management issues which may well involve substantial expenditure and in the author's view are matters for which the landlord should be responsible.

6 - 2.11.24 Inclusion of this clause effectively means that the tenant will end up funding the initial costs incurred by the landlord. This again is unacceptable for the reasons set out in paragraph 6 - 2.11.15.

6 - 2.11.25 This amendment ensures that the nuisance has to give rise to a tortious claim in damages and is more than what in every day language amounts to a nuisance in the sense of being an annoyance or interference to a third party.

SCHEDULE 7 - THE SUBJECTIONS

Those matters referred to in the register of title number CW 875823 as evidenced by office copy entries of the said title number dated the _______ day of _______ 19

SCHEDULE 7 - THE SUBJECTIONS

In an attempt to crystallise those matters to which the building is subject and subject to which, therefore, the tenant takes the premises, it is important to crystallise this by setting out the date of office copy entries on which the tenant is relying. The author would suggest that these office copy entries or at least certified copies are in fact kept with the deeds following completion of the lease.

SCHEDULE 8 - THE AUTHORISED GUARANTEE AGREEMENT

DATE [ ]

PARTIES

1. **'Guarantor'** **[(name of outgoing tenant)]** [of (address) (or as appropriate) the registered office of which is at (address)] [Company Registration number [ ]]

2. **'Landlord'** **[(name of landlord)]** [of (address) (or as appropriate) the registered office of which is at (address)] [Company Registration number [ ]]

OPERATIVE PROVISIONS

1 DEFINITIONS AND INTERPRETATION

For all purposes of this guarantee the terms defined in this clause have the meanings specified

1.1 **'Assignee'** (insert name of incoming tenant)

1.2 **'Lease'** the lease dated (date) and made between (name of original landlord) and (name of original tenant) and (name of original guarantor) for a term of (number) years commencing on and including (commencement date) [and varied by a deed dated (date) and made between (names of parties)]

1.3 **'Premises'** the premises demised by the Lease

1.4 **'Liability Period'** the period during which the Assignee is bound by the tenant covenants of the Lease

1.5 Terms from the Landlord and Tenant (Covenants) Act 1995

The expressions 'authorised guarantee agreement' and 'tenant covenants' have the same meaning in this guarantee as in the Landlord and Tenant (Covenants) Act 1995 section 28(1)

1.6 References to clauses

Any reference in this deed to a clause without further designation is to be construed as a reference to the clause of this deed so numbered

SCHEDULE 8 - THE AUTHORISED GUARANTEE AGREEMENT

As a general principle, Authorised Guarantee Agreements ('AGA's') are still very much in their infancy and there has not been much debate (and little case law) about their form or their interpretation. The majority of the amendments put forward simply mirror those referred to in the guarantor section of the main lease (clause 6).

2 RECITALS

2.1 Consent required

By clause (insert number) of the Lease, the Landlord's consent to an assignment of the Lease is required

2.2 Agreement to consent

The Landlord has agreed to give consent to the assignment to the Assignee on condition that the Guarantor enters into this guarantee

2.3 Effective time

This guarantee takes effect only when the Lease is assigned to the Assignee

3 GUARANTOR'S COVENANTS

In consideration of the Landlord's consent to the assignment, the Guarantor covenants with the Landlord and without the need for any express assignment with all his successors in title as set out in this clause 3

3.1 Payment and performance

The Assignee must punctually pay the rents reserved by the Lease and observe and perform the covenants and other terms of it throughout the Liability Period, and if at any time during the Liability Period the Assignee defaults in paying the rents or in observing or performing any of the covenants or other terms of the Lease the Guarantor must pay the rents and observe or perform the covenants or terms in respect of which the Assignee is in default, and make good to the Landlord on demand, ~~and indemnify the Landlord against~~, all reasonable foreseeable losses, damages, costs and expenses resulting from such non-payment non-performance or non-observance notwithstanding:

3.1.1 any time or indulgence granted by the Landlord to the Assignee, or any neglect or forbearance of the Landlord in enforcing the payment of the rents or the observance or performance of the covenants or other terms of the Lease, or any refusal by the Landlord to accept rents tendered by or on behalf of the Assignee at a time when the Landlord is entitled, or will after the service of a notice under the Law of Property Act 1925 section 146 be entitled, to re-enter the Premises

3.1.2 that the terms of the Lease may have been varied by agreement between the parties unless the variation is prejudicial to the Guarantor

3.1.3 that the Assignee has surrendered part of the Premises, in which event the liability of the Guarantor under the Lease is to continue in respect of the part of the Premises not surrendered after making any necessary apportionments under the Law of Property Act 1925 section 1406 and

3.1.4 anything else by which, but for this clause 3.1, the Guarantor would have been released

3.2 New lease following disclaimer

If, during the Liability Period, any trustee in bankruptcy or liquidator of the Assignee disclaims the Lease, the Guarantor must, if required by notice served by the Landlord within ~~6~~30 days of the Landlord's becoming aware of the disclaimer, take from the Landlord forthwith a lease of the Premises for the residue of the contractual term of the Lease as at the date of the disclaimer, at the rent then being paid under the Lease and subject to the same covenants and terms as in the Lease the new lease to commence on the date of the disclaimer. The Guarantor must pay the reasonable and proper costs of the new lease and execute and deliver to the Landlord a counterpart of it

3.3 Payments following disclaimer

If, during the Liability Period, the Lease is disclaimed and for any reason the Landlord does not require the Guarantor to accept a new lease of the Premises in accordance with clause 3.2, the Guarantor must pay to the Landlord on demand an amount equal to the rents reserved by the Lease for the period commencing with the date of the disclaimer and ending on whichever is the earlier of the date being ~~6~~3 months after the disclaimer the date, if any, on which the Premises are relet, and the end of the contractual term of the Lease and the Landlord covenants to use his best endeavours to relet the same

4 LANDLORD'S COVENANT

4.1 The Landlord covenants with the Guarantor that he will notify the Guarantor in writing within 7 days of being informed of the facts bringing the Liability Period to an end and will repay to the Guarantor (with interest) any sum paid for a period beyond the date on which the Liability Period comes to an end

5 SEVERANCE

5.1 Severance of void provisions

Any provision of this deed rendered void by virtue of the Landlord and Tenant (Covenants) Act 1995 section 25 is to be severed from all remaining provisions, and the remaining provisions are to be preserved

5.2 Limitation of provisions

If any provision in this deed extends beyond the limits permitted by the Landlord and Tenant (Covenants) Act 1995 section 25, that provision is to be varied so as not to extend beyond those limits

IN WITNESS whereof the parties hereto have executed this deed the date first hereinbefore written

Original/

The Common Seal of [ ])

Limited was hereunto affixed in the presence)

of:-)

....

Director

....

Secretary/Director

Counterpart/

The Common Seal of [ ])

Limited was hereunto affixed in the presence)

of:-)

....

Director

....

Secretary/Director

Index